Property

around the
World

howtobooks

Please send for a free copy of the latest catalogue:

How To Books
3 Newtec Place, Magdalen Road,
Oxford OX4 1RE, United Kingdom
mail: info@howtobooks.co.uk
http://www.howtobooks.co.uk

Property Hotspots around the World

Find the best places to invest outside the UK

Ajay Ahuja

3| 2046719

howtobooks

I dedicate this book to my mother.

Many thanks to Giles and Nikki, my family and Ellie.

An extra special thanks to Kash Uddin for his researching skills.

Published by
How To Books Ltd, 3 Newtec Place
Magdalen Road, Oxford, OX4 1RE, United Kingdom.
Tel: (01865) 793806. Fax: (01865) 248780.
email: info@howtobooks.co.uk
http://www.howtobooks.co.uk

First published in 2005

British Library Cataloguing in Publication Data
A catalogue record for this book is available from the British Library

Cover design by Baseline Arts Ltd, Oxford
Produced for How To Books by Deer Park Productions, Tavistock, Devon
Typeset by Pantek Arts Ltd, Maidstone, Kent
Printed and bound in Great Britain by Bell & Bain Ltd, Glasgow

NOTE: The material contained in this book is set out in good faith for general
guidance and no liability can be accepted for loss or expense incurred as a result
of relying in particular circumstances on statements made in the book. The laws
and regulations are complex and liable to change, and readers should check the
current position with the relevant authorities before making personal arrangements.

Contents

A Note from the Author

Over the last four years we have seen property prices in the UK more than double. There may be some more room for capital growth but the growth will be at best modest. The reason for this is the market correcting itself. Property used to be cheap! As an accountant using various asset valuation tools I was able to spot this undervaluation in the market. I was not, however, able to spot how quickly this correction would happen. With hindsight the real reason why prices have rocketed is that every lender in the UK is now offering a buy-to-let mortgage. Since the banks allowed us to fund second, third, fourth and even more properties (in my case especially!) with the rent received from the tenant it was a simple case of supply and demand – buyers exceeded properties.

Now with yields below 5%, property in most of the UK looks very unattractive. Especially with rates rising and borrowing rates in excess of 5%, novice investors are finding that there is a shortfall between the rent received and the mortgage payment. Novice investors are having to contribute out of their own pocket to meet the mortgage payment. The wise investor has been forced to abstain from the market or to travel all around the UK to find a suitable area to offer a decent return on their money. The few areas left will without a doubt dry up. This is why this book has been written. If you wish to carry on investing in property you need to go *international*!

I would rather not invest abroad if there are suitable investments in the UK. You have the barriers such as distance, language, tax and legal differences and these all have to be managed. However, I challenge any expert to present to me a better investment than property. Property is a sure way to wealth. It is the only investment that you can gear up to 85% Loan To Value, be funded by someone else (i.e. the tenant) and requires little effort from yourself. You can duplicate the process as many times as you like without restriction. So the barriers are worth overcoming as there is no other asset investment that can compete with property.

The hotspots I have chosen give you a good spread of the world. It makes an enjoyable read purely from a general knowledge point of view. If you read deeper into each hotspot you can see that each one is worth a visit based on the financial fundamentals. It would make a great trip based on any fundamentals! I would suggest you use the internet to gain further knowledge of each hotspot. If possible invest in a few overseas phone calls to agents out there. You can gauge a lot from just speaking to the locals.

I hope you enjoy the book. It will certainly make you feel like going on holiday. If you wish to make contact with me then visit www.buytolethotspots.com or email me at ajay@propertyhotspots.net.

Good luck

Ajay Ahuja

Acknowledgements

About the researcher

Having spent much of my time providing the business scope, I must state that I am indebted to the research input offered by a colleague. I would like to thank Kashim Uddin for his immeasurable efforts. His hard work and persistence has seen the project through from start to finish. Having recently completed a research-based Masters degree in the sciences, his well-honed analytical skills and versatile creative input have been of huge importance in the delivery of this book. Still in his infancy of business appreciation, his enthusiasm for this book has been more than welcome and we'll hopefully see some more of his work in the near future.

About the contributor

Lee Connolly was instrumental in helping to choose the hot spots for this book. He bought his first overseas home in Torrevieja, Spain in 1985 for only £14,000. Having spent all his working life in the financial services industry, he knew it was a sound investment and has a portfolio of properties in the Costa Blanca and Costa Calida. It was through this success and knowledge that Spanish Property Centre was established.

During the last five years, Lee has increased his portfolio to purchase in Florida, financed at competitive rates to fund Rent Guarantee programmes. This is continuing. Also for middle to long term capital growth Lee has purchased in Cyprus North and South, and is building a portfolio in the emerging markets of Eastern Europe, covering those countries which have recently joined the European Union and those with strong chances of joining in 2007.

Many individuals and small investor groups are looking at redistributing investments held in the UK to the overseas market and, given the risk and reward strategy of a good spread of a balanced portfolio, the returns are looking very promising.

Since 1981, Lee Connolly Financial Services (now Limited), has been successfully arranging mortgages for clients in the UK. Many clients have remortgaged to raise funds to purchase their overseas property, often using a drawdown facility. It was a natural progression for Lee to branch out into the overseas mortgage market, offering mortgage products in many countries with self-certifiation schemes at 75% of the purchase price and in some cases 80% with rates often lower than in the UK. These are innovative, unique schms such as mortgage finance in Northern Cyprus and 80% mortgages in Spain which do not take into account the buyer's UK expenditure, i.e. mortgages, loans and credit cards which in some cases can be restrictive.

Once again the compay has progressed to include another sister company, European Car Hire Limited, which provides very competitive rates for car hire. These companies have come together under one umbrella to form C Group.

For further information please call and quote CGPI to obtain a discount on their fees.

International Property Sales Limited	0845 600 8866
Spanish Property Centre	01279 454644
Lee Connolly Financial Services Limited	01279 626500
European Car Hire Limited	0845 601 4891

What is a Hotspot?

A hotspot is an area where there are properties available for sale that fall into one of these categories:

Category	Description
Gold	Property prices are predicted to rise at a greater rate than the national average *and* the rental yield is greater than the national average. This is the most desirable category as it enjoys the best of both worlds – capital growth and yield, thus spreading the return and overall risk.
Silver	The rental yield is greater than the national average. It is ranked second as the yield is a certain outcome.
Bronze	Property prices are predicted to rise at a greater rate than the national average. However, capital growth is an uncertain outcome.

In our experience investors choose category Gold, Silver or Bronze according to personal circumstances but particularly on gut reaction. Our advice is to choose all of them! There is no need to place all your eggs in one basket. Property is a relatively safe investment but there is a degree of uncertainty, so if possible, by investing in all the categories above, you eliminate some of the business risk.

Identifying a hotspot
So how did we identify the hotspots listed? The categories are based on two factors:

1. Actual rental yields.
2. Predicted property prices.

1. Actual rental yields

The first factor, actual rental yields, was easy to do. Actual rental yield is:

$$\frac{\text{ACTUAL YEARLY RENT}}{\text{ACTUAL PROPERTY PRICE}} \times 100$$

Since these figures are actuals, we collated all the rental figures from the local letting agents in the chosen location. All the local property prices come from our research on the internet. We calculated all the yields being offered from each city based on the equation above. We then eliminated all the poor yielding locations, where we thought tenant demand was low (even if they were high yielding) and all political high risk countries.

2. Predicted property prices

Here we did not predict property prices as this is an impossible thing to do. If we could do this we would not be writing this book but buying everything we could in a hotspot area! All we did was to look at what would make an area's property price rise above the UK average. We came up with the following:

- Proposed transportation link improvements such as improved road and rail links, expansion of local airports and improved public transport.
- Proposed inward investment from private companies, government and trusts.
- Proposed improvements to leisure facilities such as sport centres, parks and shopping centres.
- Higher than average yields.
- Recent increases in political stability.
- The likelihood of holiday seasons being lengthened for holiday areas.
- Our own experience gathered from being in this industry and from comments from letting and estate agents.

The Seven Types of Investor

What type of investor am I?

So you know you want to invest in property but why and how are you going to? There are many ways to invest in property but we have narrowed these down to seven types. Investors can be broadly categorised into one of the following and it is up to you to decide which category or categories you fit into.

Type	Objective	Description
Cash and equity investor	To maximise rental income and capital growth combined. Will also sell home when this further achieves this objective.	This approach is a semi-business approach. The investor has no love for the property but is only interested in the overall money it is going to make. They will sell if the market is high or hold if the rental income is good. Their intention is to re-invest any monies gained into another property or properties. This type of investor will have a greater degree of interest in property than other investors as they will stay abreast of the market.
Pension investor	To cover all costs involved with the house by the rental income and have the house paid off by retirement age. The rental income (or return on sale) thus provides an income.	This investor will be at least 15 years off retirement age. They will look for a property that will always have good rental demand as they intend to live off this rental income when they retire. They may also consider selling the property and using the monies raised to purchase an annuity. If so, they will also look for a high capital growth area. As good practice this type of investor should always evaluate whether their equity in the property can purchase an income greater than the rental income currently being generated.

▶

Type	Objective	Description
Holiday investor	To cover some of the costs of owning the house by letting it out but ultimately to get a holiday home that can be enjoyed by family and friends.	Typically an investor with a family who wishes to save on holiday costs and to eventually pass down the property to their children, or release the value of their nest egg. Saving money rather than making money is the motivation for this investor. They will seek non-conventional investment properties such as cottages, properties far from the city centre and stations and restricted occupancy homes.
Retirement investor	To cover all costs involved with the house by the rental income and have the house paid off by retirement age. Then sell own home to move into the investment home.	Again non-typical investment properties will be sought and they will probably seek properties in a surrounding village of a main town or city. A key concern for this investor is tenant demand so they may well be steered towards villages surrounding main towns and cities. The investor will use the proceeds from the sale of their original home to clear outstanding mortgages and purchase an annuity.
University investor	To provide a home for son/daughter while at university for three years. Sell/hold after three years.	The aim of this investor is to purchase a four+ bedroomed home near the university and get the son or daughter to live in one room and rent the other rooms to his or her friends. The rental income will cover all costs involved with the house and then the house can be sold on for profit or held and rented out again through the university. The overall profit on the investment is the boarding fees saved in the three years and the gain on the sale of the property.
Downshifter investor	To sell existing home and buy a lifestyle property (e.g. B&B) with no outstanding mortgage.	This investor will realise the gain in their home free from tax and purchase a property which will change both their location and their job. Typical properties are B&Bs and shops with living accommodation above.

▶

Type	Objective	Description
Business investor	To maximise rental income to replace salary from full-time employment.	The investor will look for high yielding properties so as to replace the lost income from leaving their job. They will invest in only high tenant demand areas as they rely on this income to pay day-to-day bills. They will be interested in the property market and hence will be abreast of the latest prices, mortgage rates and rental figures. This way they can ensure that their net income is maximised.

From reading this list you will be able to decide what type of investor you are and more importantly what you want to get from your investment. Once you are clear what you want then the whole process becomes easier as you know exactly what you are looking for.

Property Hotspots

This section gives details for each hotspot we have found. Here is a brief description about what each listing describes.

Country, City		
Country data		
Population	Population of country	
Population growth	Growth in population of the country	
Land area	The land area of the country in square kilometres	
Currency and currency rate	The currency of the country and its conversion rate to the UK pound	
GDP-PPP method	The Gross Domestic Prouct based on Purchasing Power Parity which elimates absolute price distortions	
GDP growth	The growth in GDP year on year	
GDP per head	The GDP per person in the country	
Financial	**Interest rate:** The bank of the coutry's base rate	**Inflation rate:** The inflation rate calculated according to the method of the country
National Bank	The bank of the country	
Political	Description of the political climate	
Social security	Whether social security exists	
Languages	Languages commonly spoken in the country	
Customaries	Specific customaries relevant to the country	
Ethnic make-up	The split of different ethnicities within the country	
Tax	**Income Tax** The Income Tax rules for the country	**Capital Gains Tax** The Capital Gains Tax rules for the country
Description	A general description of the country	

▶

Local data				
Investor profile	Typical investor suited to the hotspot			
Category	A rating based on the hotspot's capital growth and yield prospects			
Population	**Total** Population of the hotspot		**British** British population of the hotspot	
Climate	**Hours of sunshine per day in summer**	**Average rainfall per year**	**Average temperature January**	**Average temperature July**	**Average water temperature**
	Self-explanatory	Self-explanatory	Average temperature for that month	Average temperature for that month	Self-explanatory
Proximity to	**Airport:** Name and distance from closest airport **Beach:** Distance from beach **Nearest city:** Name of closest city			
Restaurants and bars	What to do in the evening			
Sports and leisure facilities	What to do in the day			
Transport	**Public transport:** Description of public transport **Roads:** Description of road network			
Crime rate	An indication of crime levels			
Main types of employment	Self-explanatory			
Future plans	Future plans for the hotspot			
Yield range	The range of yields to be expected from prospective property purchases			
Type of property	**Entry price**	**Rent – peak**	**Rent – off peak**	**Average annual yield**
2 bed apartment **3 bed apartment** **3 bed townhouse** **Detached**	The lowest prices found for each type of property	The rent per calendar month in the peak season	The rent per calendar month in the off-peak season	The yield, being the mid price of the monthly rental multiplied by 12 and divided by the purchase price expressed as a percentage
Demand for letting	**Peak** Self-explanatory		**Off peak** Self-explanatory	
Finance and leisure scores	**Financial** (out of 5) Score out of 5 based on its ability to make you money	**Leisure** (out of 5) Score out of 5 based on the amount of enjoyment you can expect	**Total** (out of 10) Total of financial and leisure	

▶

Flights scheduled from	Airports in the UK that fly to the hotspot	
Typical cost of flights	Peak Self-explanatory	Off Peak Self-explanatory
Operators	Operators that fly to the hotspot	
Description	General description of the hotspot and why we think it's a hotspot	
Hot website	A website to visit to gain further knowledge about the hotspot	
Estate agents:		
Name	Address	Tel	Web
Name address, telephone and web details for estate agents selling properties in the hotspot		
Letting agents:		
Name	Address	Tel	Web
Name address, telephone and web details for estate agents selling properties in the hotspot		

Property Hotspot List

Africa

Egypt, El Gouna, Red Sea
Ghana, Accra
South Africa, Natal Midlands

Egypt, El Gouna, Red Sea

Country data

Population	69.54 million
Population growth	1.72%
Land area	995,450 sq km
Currency and exchange rate	1 Egyptian pound = 100 piasters (~0.088 GBP)
GDP-PPP method	US$203,313.0 millions
GDP growth	1.55%
GDP per head	US$2,924.0 thousands per person

Financial	Interest rate 10%	Inflation rate 4.0%

National bank	Central Bank of Egypt
Political	President Hosni Mubarak assumed power on President Sadat's assassination by political extremists in 1981 and won a six-year presidential term in 1999 after 93.97% of voters approved his candidacy. He discarded many of the unpopular features of Sadat's domestic policies and placed great emphasis on economic reform. The government has faced regular upheavals from Islamic and political extremists since the early 1990s. On some occasions foreigners have been targeted and the worst case was in 1997 when 58 tourists, six of them British, were murdered. The Egyptian authorities have quelled much of the violence, with hundreds of militants killed or subdued but its complete eradication is not yet in sight. Extremists have unsuccessfully targeted Hosni Mubarak on a few occasions. The government has to address the economic problems which underlie extremism.
Social security	Yes
Languages	Arabic (official); English and French widely understood by educated classes
Customaries	With Islam being the dominant influence, many traditional and customary beliefs are prevalent throughout the country. The people are generally welcoming and courteous, expecting similar attitudes from visitors. Handshaking will suffice as a greeting. Traditional conservative clothing is the general attire for men and women and this should be especially observed when in a religious or holy setting. Western style of clothing is accepted in modern nightclubs, restaurants, hotels and bars in the capital, Cairo. Smoking is very common.
Ethnic make-up	Eastern Hemitic stock 99.0%; Greek, Nubian, Armenian, and other Europeans 1.0%

Tax	Income Tax		Capital Gains Tax
	Non-resident individuals and are expatriate experts (as defined) generally taxed on Egyptian-source income only. Taxes are withheld from salaries at a rate of 20% on salary income up to LE 50,000 per year, and at a rate of 32% on the excess.		Capital gains derived from transfers of real estate are not subject to tax unless the real estate is used in a trade or business. However, a 2.5% tax is levied on the gross proceeds from the disposal of urban land and buildings, regardless of usage.

Individual:

Taxable income (LE)		Tax rate
Exceeding (LE)	Not exceeding (LE)	%
0	2,500	20
2,500	7,000	27
7,000	16,000	35
16,000	–	40

Description	Egypt is one of the most populated regions in the Arab region and is the second most populous in Africa after Nigeria. The economic stabilisation and reform brought it on track. Ongoing reduction of debts in addition to good budgets have contributed to this progress. Egypt is heavily import-dependent. Exports include petrochemicals, oil and cotton. The tourism industry has experienced some deceleration due to the current events in the Middle East and possible security concerns. However, it is still providing a good source of revenue in addition to other service jobs and emigrant workers' remittances.

Local data				
Investor profile	Cash & equity investor; pension investor; holiday investor; retirement investor; downshifter investor; business investor			
Category	Gold			

Population	Total 50,000		British 3000	

Climate	Hours of sunshine per day in summer	Average rainfall per year	Average temperature January	Average temperature July	Average water temperature
	12	14 days	21°C	33°C	25°C

Proximity to	**Airport:** Fly direct to Cairo then either take an internal flight to El Gouna Airport or go overland by bus or by car. Alternatively flights are also available to Hurghada airport which is half an hour away from El Gouna.

▶

	Beach: Zeytuna Beach, Mangroovy Beach **Nearest city:** Hurghada
Restaurants and bars	El Gouna has dozens of nightspots offering a variety of atmospheres and entertainment with a huge selection of restaurants, bars, pubs, discos and casinos, from international guest DJs, to concerts, trendy bars, cozy pubs and even oriental shows.
Sports and leisure facilities	World class scuba diving, 18 hole USPGA championship golf course, desert safaris, kite surfing, water-skiing, horseback and camel riding, boat excursions to uninhabited islands, sailing, spas and fitness centres.
Transport	**Public transport:** El Gouna's on-call taxi service makes it easy to get around El Gouna, the surrounding Red Sea area or even all of Egypt from Alexandria to Aswan. Internal bus network in addition to buses to and from Cairo daily. **Roads:** Desert roads – driving has special requirements. Be sure to get a suitable vehicle and guidance on possible hazards.
Crime rate	Very low, considerably safer than other regions of Egypt.
Main types of employment	Tourism and services
Future plans	Investments are being made in order to prepare the airport for expansion so that it can cater for international charter through 2005.
Yield range	15–22%

Type of property	Entry price	Rent – peak	Rent – off peak	Average annual yield
2 bed apartment	£15,000	£300	£250	22%
3 bed apartment	£23,000	£350	£300	16%
3 bed townhouse	£27,000	£350	£300	14%
Detached	£32,000	£400	£400	15%

Demand for letting	Peak Very high		Off peak High	

Finance and leisure scores	**Financial** (out of 5) 5	**Leisure** (out of 5) 4	**Total** (out of 10) 9

Flights scheduled from	London Heathrow, London Gatwick and most other major cities in the UK. At least one connecting flight is usually required.

Typical cost of flights	Peak £300–700	Off peak £200–500

Operators	Most European tour operators and travel agencies offer booking for El Gouna. El Gouna Travel Agency (+20 65) 580 085 / 86 protours@orascom.net Egypt Air, Air France, British Airways, KLM, Lufthansa. Charter services fly direct from London Gatwick to Egypt. British Mediterranean (a franchise partner of British Airways) operates daily services from London to Alexandria. Egypt Air also operates internal flights.

▶

Description	Under the silhouettes of sharp edged mountains and bordering the crystal waters of the Red Sea lies El Gouna, the region's most exclusive destination. Built on clusters of islands surrounded by turquoise lagoons, El Gouna spreads over 11 kilometres of the most pristine beachfront.
	There is a higher than average British population compared to the rest of the country. Yields are very high and sustainable throughout the year. There is little or no tax payable on disposal of investment properties so you can exit with a small charge.
	This area has a lot to catch up to hence prices are cheap. Do not expect to get a pretty looking property unless you want you want to pay double the entry price. Again the war has made this area a moderate risk as opposed to a low risk but in the long term it's a safe bet.
	The interest rate is high at 10% but the yields compensate for this. Interest rates are set to come down as inflation rates are sensible thus increasing the profit margin on an investment property.
Hot website	www.elgouna.com

Estate agents:

Name	Address	Tel	Web
El Gouna Real Estate for International Clientele			www.redsea-realestate.com elgouna@redsea-realestate.com
Sharm El Sheikh & Hurghada Apartments and Villas			www.red-sea-guide.com/real-estate/ info@red-sea-guide.com
Real Estate Egypt	49, El-Makrizy St, Heliopolis, Cairo 11341	202 4530456	realestate.egypt.com/
First Class Egypt	8 Adan St, Al Mohandiseen, Cairo	202 3369095	www.1classegypt.com

Letting agents:

Name	Address	Tel	Web
Real Estate Egypt	49, El-Makrizy St, Heliopolis, Cairo 11341	202 4530456	realestate.egypt.com/
First Class Egypt	8 Adan St, Al Mohandiseen, Cairo	202 3369095	www.1classegypt.com

Ghana, Accra

Country data

Population	19.89 million
Population growth	1.85%
Land area	230,020 sq km
Currency and exchange rate	1 new cedi (C) = 100 pesewas (~0.0000607260 GBP)
GDP-PPP method	US$35,918.0 millions
GDP growth	2.31%
GDP per head	US$1,805.0 thousands per person

Financial	Interest rate 24.5%	Inflation rate 14.5%

National bank	Bank of Ghana
Political	Since reforms in 1992, the President and a National Assembly are elected. The current President, John Kufour, was sworn in in January 2001. Ghana is now an African success story. It has a pluralistic political system. The strength of this was underlined by the elections held as described above, when, for the first in its history, Ghana witnessed the election of an opposition party. What followed was a smooth transition of power. In 2002 President Kufour established a commission charged with examining human rights violations that occurred during the military rule period. Ghana's contributions to United Nations peacekeeping is highly renowned and dates back to 1960.
Social security	Ghana does not impose social security tax. However, employers must withhold 5% of each employee's pay and contribute 12.5% of each employee's pay to the Social Security and National Insurance Trust.
Languages	English (official); indigenous African languages (including Asante Twi, Akuapim Twi, Fante, Ewe, Ga-Adangme, Nzema, Dagbani, Dagaari, Kasem, Frafra, Buli, Kusaal, Sisaala, Gonja)
Customaries	Special events: Ghanaian festivals are well worth seeing with drumming, dancing and feasting. Every part of the country has its own annual festivals for the affirmation of tribal values, the remembrance of ancestors and past leaders, and the purification of the state in preparation for another year. Local dress includes the expensive, hand-woven Kente cloth for which Ghana is famous: this is worn by men like a toga. Social conventions: Ghanaians should always be addressed by their formal titles unless they specifically request otherwise. Handshaking is the usual form of greeting. It is customary in much of West Africa not to use the left hand for touching food. Photography: permission should be sought before photographing military installations, government buildings or airports.
Ethnic make-up	Moshi-Dagomba; Akan; Ewe; Ga; Gurma; Yoruba; European; Other

▶

Tax	Income Tax				Capital Gains Tax
	Taxable income (c)		Tax on lower amount	Rate on excess	Capital gains are taxed at a rate of 10%. Capital losses are not taken into account.
	Exceeding (c)	Not exceeding (c)	(c)	%	
	0	1,200,000	0	0	
	1,200,000	2,400,000	0	5	
	2,400,000	5,400,000	60,000	10	
	5,400,000	24,000,000	360,000	15	
	24,000,000	48,000,000	3,150,000	20	
	48,000,000	–	7,950,000	30	

Non-residents are subject to income tax at a flat rate of 20%.
   Management fees and technical service fees paid to non-residents are subject to a 20% final withholding tax.

Description	Agriculture occupies most of the working population, producing both subsistence and cash crops. Cocoa is a major economic source and Ghana is one of the world's biggest producers. Other sources of economic benefit are timber and gold mining. Fishing has grown in importance since the acquisition of shipping vessels. Major trading partners: the UK, US, France, Italy, Nigeria and Togo. Member of the Economic Community of West African States (ECOWAS). Kufuor tackled an economy that was dipping. Tough measures included raising fuel duties by 90%. The recovery in the price of gold and cocoa helped Ghana reach macro-economic stability. Whilst poverty is declining, unemployment still remains around 17%.

Local data

Investor profile	Cash & equity investor; pension investor; holiday investor; retirement investor; downshifter investor; business investor
Category	Bronze

Population	Total	British
	1,605,400	5,000

Climate	Hours of sunshine per day in summer	Average rainfall per year	Average temperature January	Average temperature July	Average water temperature
	9	Annual rainfall in the capital averages 865mm. Wettest month is June when rainfall averages 235mm	27°C/ 80°F	24.6°C/ 76.3°F	20°C

▶

Proximity to	**Airport:** Kotoka International Airport is Ghana's only airport. It is situated on the outskirts of Accra. The flight time between London and Ghana is approximately $6\frac{1}{2}$ hours.
	Beach: Accra's beaches are another big draw, but the best ones are all a few kilometres outside of town. Coco Beach, east of Nungua, is accessible by tro-tro, but the nicest ones to the west all require private transport. The best beach in Accra to visit is the Labadi Pleasure Beach.
	Nearest city: Tema, Nsawam, Oda, Winneba

Restaurants and bars	Accra is famous throughout West Africa for its vibrant nightlife, especially its dance clubs, which centre around Nkrumah Circle. Rasta togs and dreadlocks usually mark the entrance to the hippest spots.
	    In addition to the bars and restaurants in hotels, there is a wide range of restaurants offering menus to suit many different palates with food generally of a good standard. Eating out is generally less expensive than in the UK. French cuisine tends to be more expensive. There are also many snack bars (locally known as chop bars) and shops, where good quality Ghanaian food is sold at reasonable prices.
	    There are a few fast food restaurants opening in Osu (an area of Accra frequented by expatriates and middle income Ghanaians) but the recognised chains have yet to establish a presence.

Sports and leisure facilities	Compared to other African countries, Ghana's national parks and game reserves are small, and relatively few tourists visit them.
	    Although Ghana's coast offers miles of sandy beaches, strong currents and tides can make bathing quite dangerous. Near Accra there are three swimming pools near the surf. Sailing or water-skiing offers alternatives and there are numerous centres with good facilities. The best spots for surfing are at Fete, Dixcove (both west of Accra) and Kokrobite near Accra. Another exhilarating experience is to be taken out over the surf in a local fishing boat.
	    Ghanaians are fanatical followers of football and very interested in tennis and boxing. Another popular sport is horseracing, which takes place at the Accra racecourse every Saturday. There are golf courses at Accra.

Transport	**Public transport:** Most Ghanaians get around in taxis, tro-tros (minibuses) and mammy wagons (generally some sort of converted pickup truck). Government-run buses connect most major towns and some smaller ones, but their service isn't what it used to be and it's usually better to travel with any of the private bus companies. A comfortable but slow railway system connects Accra, Kumasi and Takoradi in a single-track triangle. **Roads:** Ghana's road network is in decent shape, though there are some badly potholed stretches and almost all secondary roads are unsealed. Car rental is expensive but available in Accra.
Crime rate	Accra has its share of crime, though it is generally regarded as being relatively safe and peaceful. Lately, however, the rate of crime seems to be rising. The police are working hard to arrest the situation. Be careful of pickpockets and armed robbers.

Main types of employment	The sale of anything whatsoever in a market, petty trading, hawking or selling from a kiosk at any place; operation of a taxi service and car hire service (a non-Ghanaian may undertake this service provided he has a minimum fleet of ten new vehicles); all aspects of pool betting business and lotteries, except football pools; operation of beauty salons and barber shops.			
Future plans	Ghana will spend between 100 and 150 million dollars to upgrade facilities at the Accra and Kumasi sports stadiums as well as the construction of new ones in Sekondi and Tamale.			
Yield range	7–9 %			
Type of property	Entry price	Rent – peak	Rent – off peak	Average annual yield
2 bed apartment	£13,000	£100	£100	9.2%
3 bed apartment	£18,000	£120	£120	8%
3 bed townhouse	£20,000	£130	£130	7.8%
Detached	£23,000	£150	£150	7.8%
Demand for letting	Peak High		Off peak Moderately low	
Finance and leisure scores	Financial (out of 5) 3	Leisure (out of 5) 2	Total (out of 10) 5	
Flights scheduled from	There are Ghana Airways flights from Kotoka Airport in Accra to almost every country in West Africa, as well as flights to New York and London. British Airways flies from London Heathrow to Accra and Ghana Airways flies from London Heathrow to Accra three times a week.			
Typical cost of flights	Peak £800–1800		Off peak £490–1100	
Operators	British Airways and Ghana Airways, SN Brussels (Brussels), Alitalia (Rome), Saudia (Rome), KLM (Amsterdam) and Egypt Airlines (Cairo), Ethiopian Airlines (Addis Abeba).			
Description	Accra has friendly people, wonderful beaches, good food and a great atmosphere. Accra is the capital of Ghana; it's a busy, smelly, vibrant city. Accra is not a city made for tourism – it's a living, working, breathing city where Ghanaians work and party, especially during the weekend. However, as a tourist, you will be made very welcome; but as always it's best to try to blend in. This area is another cash buy. Have you seen the interest rate – 24.5% ouch! However, due to the popularity of this area as a resort for the holidaymaker looking for something different, property prices have to rise. Expect to sell to another holidaymaker soon catching wind of the rapid growth in prices. They too will be cash buyers so there will be a limit to the selling price, say £75,000 max in a few years.			
Hot website	www.accra.com			

Estate agents:			
Name	Address	Tel	Web
Waeco Properties	No. 16. 4th Circular Road Cantonments, PO Box 632, Accra	+233 (021) 775570	www.waecoproperties. com info@waecoproperties. com
ASV Homes	PO Box 244, Legon, Accra	+233 021 512 781, +233 027 603 324	www.asvhomes.com sales@asvhomes.com
New England Estates Ltd		+233 21 222202	www.newengland. com.gh/ newengland@ ghana.com
Punch Ghana	C485/14 Nii Bone Cr., Dzorwula, Accra P.M.B. 183, Accra-North	+233 24320476	www.ghanahouse.com
Letting agents:			
Name	Address	Tel	Web
Punch Ghana	C485/14 Nii Bone Cr., Dzorwula, Accra PMB 183, Accra-North	+233 24320476	www.ghanahouse.com
ASV Homes	PO Box 244, Legon, Accra	+233 021 512 781 +233 027 603 324	www.asvhomes.com sales@asvhomes.com

South Africa, Natal Midlands

Country data

Population	43.59 million
Population growth	0.380 %
Land area	1,219,912 sq km
Currency and exchange rate	1 rand (R$) = 100 cents (~0.0866 GBP)
GDP-PPP method	US$292,983.0 millions
GDP growth	1.81 %
GDP per head	US$6,722.0 thousands per person

Financial	Interest rate 13.5%	Inflation rate 7.9%

National bank	South African Reserve Bank
Political	Under the terms of the new constitution, legislative power is vested in a bicameral parliament, comprising a National Assembly and a National Council of Provinces. The parliamentary and presidential elections of April 2004 were the third since the end of Apartheid with the ANC taking 70% of the votes. The Democratic Alliance proved to be the biggest challengers to the ANC.
Social security	Yes (limited)
Languages	Afrikaans, English, Ndebele, Pedi, Sotho, Swazi, Tsonga, Tswana, Venda, Xhosa, Zulu
Customaries	Handshaking is the usual form of greeting. Normal courtesies should be shown when visiting someone's home. Smoking is prohibited in public buildings and on public transport. Visitors should also bear in mind that in certain parts of the country strong racist attitudes still prevail. It is best not to get involved in political discussions. You should also remember not to photograph security institutions.
Ethnic make-up	South Asian Indian; mixed; European; indigenous African

Tax	Income Tax				Capital Gains Tax
	Taxable income (€)		Tax on lower amount	Rate on excess	From 10/2001, capital gains were taxable in south Africa. This tax is imposed through the income tax system.
	Exceeding (€)	Not exceeding (€)	(€)	%	
	0	40,000	0	18	
	40,000	80,000	7,200	25	
	80,000	110,000	17,200	30	
	110,000	170,000	26,200	35	
	170,000	240,000	47,200	38	
	240,000	–	73,800	40	

▶

Description	South Africa is the world's largest producer of platinum, gold and chromium. Other major industries: automobile assembly, machinery, textile, iron and steel, chemicals, manufacturing. Major trading partners: the US, UK, Germany and Japan. One of the biggest growers of economic output is the increase in tourism. The diversified economy is largely based on the abundance of minerals.
	The government has designed a scheme under which major economic assets – notably the mines – will be transferred to 'black empowerment entities' over a ten-year period.
	Since 1998 South Africa has reversed poor growth rates and has embarked on a period of sustained growth with low to moderate inflation, a manageable debt burden and a robust growth in exports. The economy recovered quickly after being knocked off track in 2002. However, social and equality problems remain and crime is still unacceptably high. Perhaps the greatest long-term problem, especially as regards its impact on the workforce, is the very high level of HIV/AIDS infection in the country.

Local data				
Investor profile	Cash & equity investor; pension investor; holiday investor; retirement investor; downshifter investor; business investor			
Category	Gold			

Population	Total 400,000		British 300	

Climate	Hours of sunshine per day in summer	Average rainfall per year	Average temperature January	Average temperature July	Average water temperature
	7	22 days	28°C	23°C	22°C

Proximity to	**Airport:** Durban Louis Botha International airport is 2 hours drive.
	Beach: Warner beach, Tongaat Beach
	Nearest city: Durban

Restaurants and bars	Many coffee shops, tea gardens, country pubs, restaurants, wine cellars and breweries. From cosy fireside corners in pubs that make their own beers and serve hot, delicious food, to snug coffee shops serving tortes, cakes and sticky puddings – a wealth of choice.

Sports and leisure facilities	Trout fishing, golf, eco-tourism activities, hill walking, game viewing and birding, fishing, wing shooting, horse riding and polo. Natal coast is also renowned for its excellent diving and sport fishing facilities.

Transport	**Public transport:** Good public transport available. A good bus network means you can easily get to other towns, farms and beaches.
	Roads: Most roads are paved and good and the unpaved roads are also good to drive. Easy access to other towns and Durban.

Crime rate	Low

▶

Main types of employment	Predominantly farming, catering and services			
Future plans	In recent years the popularity of the Midlands Meander has created an increased demand for properties suitable for use by artists and craftworkers or for conversion to country restaurants, guesthouses or wedding and conference venues. The high concentration of excellent private schools in the area has also motivated many parents to invest in property in the Midlands. Despite an average 20 % increase in the price of good homes in the area over the past year, and a more negative view of property investment because of the higher interest rates, demand is still strong – and being helped by an increasing number of foreign visitors, mainly from the UK, Germany and Norway.			
Yield range	16–20%			
Type of property	Entry price	Rent – peak	Rent – off peak	Average annual yield
2 bed apartment	£12,000	£200	£200	20%
3 bed apartment	£15,000	£210	£210	16.8%
3 bed townhouse	£17,000	£280	£280	19.7%
Detached	£19,000	£290	£290	18.3%
Demand for letting	**Peak** High		**Off peak** High	
Finance and leisure scores	**Financial** (out of 5) 5	**Leisure** (out of 5) 4	**Total** (out of 10) 4	
Flights scheduled from	London Airports, Manchester, Birmingham, Cardiff, Edinburgh and some other major cities			
Typical cost of flights	**Peak** £600–1000		**Off peak** £400–600	
Operators	Air France, KLM, Swiss, South African Airways			
Description	Rising in the south towards the majestic Drakensberg range, this unspoilt upland area of hills, woods, lakes and streams is reminiscent of the Scottish Highlands. It is recognised as one of the most beautiful, peaceful and secure areas of Southern Africa with the rolling hills of Natal complementing the tropical coastline with its lush vegetation, warm ocean and almost year round sunshine. I recommend to buy these properties for cash, wait for the interest rates to fall to a sensible level, watch the capital value grow and then SELL! The only way is up when you look at the entry prices. Something has to go seriously wrong for you to lose money in this area. As the political stability increases so does your capital! This will be the catalyst that will cause prices to rocket – get in early.			
Hot website	www.midlandstourism.co.za/			

Estate agents:			
Name	Address	Tel	Web
Denton-Miller estates	PO Box 603, Howick 3290	(033) 330 7304	denton.miller@ mweb.co.za http://natal-country-estates.co.za
Peta Parker Properties		033-7011341/2	www.ppproperties. co.za
Pat Acutt, Acutts	460 Ridge Road, 4001, PO Box 50093, Durban 4062	031 2098111	http://www.acutts. co.za/
Remax Midlands Real Estate	PO Box 1182, Pietermaritzburg 3200,	033 345 8256	www.remax midlands.co.za
Letting agents:			
Name	Address	Tel	Web
Remax Midlands Real Estate	PO Box 1182, Pietermaritzburg 3200,	033 345 8256	www.remax midlands.co.za
Denton-Miller Estates	PO Box 603, Howick 3290	(033) 330 7304	denton.miller@ mweb.co.za http://natal-country-estates.co.za

Asia

Sri Lanka, Unawatuna, Galle
Thailand, Phuket, Pattaya
United Arab Emirates, Dubai

Sri Lanka, Unawatuna, Galle

Country data	
Population	19.41 million
Population growth	0.880%
Land area	64,740 sq km
Currency and exchange rate	1 Sri Lankan rupees (SLRe$) = 100 cents (~0.00547217 GBP)
GDP-PPP method	US$49,420.0 millions
GDP growth	−2.260%
GDP per head	US£2,546.0 thousands per person

Financial	Interest rate 15% E	Inflation rate 8.8%
National bank	Central Bank of Sri Lanka	
Political	After independence from Britain in 1948, the political scene has been dominated by two parties – the United National Party (UNP) and the Sri Lanka Freedom Party (SLFP). The country became a republic in 1972, adopting a new constitution along with the Sinhala name, Sri Lanka. Serious conflict arose from the Tamil minority's demands for a separate Tamil state, with terrorist activity by the Liberation Tigers of Tamil Eelam (Tamil Eelam being the title of their notional independent state) prevalent since the 1970s. This conflict has been of much focus for continuing governments and is still ongoing.	
Social security	Yes	
Languages	Sinhala (official and national language), Tamil (national language)	
Customaries	Shaking hands is the normal form of greeting. It is customary to be offered tea when visiting and it is considered impolite to refuse. Punctuality is appreciated. A small token of appreciation, such as a souvenir from home or company, is always welcomed. Informal, Western dress is suitable. Visitors should be decently clothed when visiting any place of worship, and shoes and hats must be removed.	
Ethnic make-up	Sinhalese 74.0%; Tamil 18.0%; Moor 7.0%; Burgher, Malay, and Vedda 1.0%	

Tax	Income Tax		Capital Gains Tax
	Taxable income (Rs)	Tax rate	From March 2002, the tax on capital gains was abolished and so was the transfer tax payable by foreign nationals on the purchase of immovable property in April 2002. However, the stamp duty on the transfer of immovable property continues to apply.
	Exceeding (Rs) / Not exceeding (Rs)	%	
	0 180,000	10	
	180,000 360,000	20	
	360,000 –	35	

Description	The Sri Lankan economy is one of the most progressive in South East Asia. Major industries: agriculture, forestry, fishing, services, manufacturing and construction. Despite the well documented internal conflicts concerning Tamil, Sri Lanka has been characterised by its steady, albeit slow, economic growth. This is reflected in the average annual growth during the last five years – between 3 and 6%, while both inflation and unemployment have been considerably reduced. The main destinations of exports: the US and UK, Belgium, Germany and the UAE.

Local data

Investor profile	Cash & equity investor; pension investor; holiday investor; retirement investor; downshifter investor; business investor
Category	Bronze

Population	Total 100,000	British 500

Climate	Hours of sunshine per day in summer	Average rainfall per year	Average temperature January	Average temperature July	Average water temperature
	9	30 days	20°C	34°C	24°C

Proximity to	**Airport:** Most visitors to Unawatuna make a beeline here from the BI Airport, Colombo, which is 150 kms away but would take over four hours by private vehicle or longer by public transport. **Beach:** Plenty of beautiful beaches in the surrounding area **Nearest city:** Galle
Restaurants and bars	Visitors expecting 24 hour beach parties and lively bars will be seriously disappointed. Thailand this ain't! The expected rise in younger tourists and backpackers will no doubt liven things up a bit but Unawatuna is a sleepy fishing village and the beach area is only mildly more awake. When the sun goes down things get very quiet – there are still plenty of bars and restaurants open (some even turn the music up!) but by midnight most have closed. There are a couple of places to hang out till the early hours but it's like being in a normal bar rather than a party. There are plenty of restaurants, with fish being very popular of course. Butter fish, calamari, prawns and lobster too.
Sports and leisure facilities	Unawatuna is a bird watcher's paradise. In addition there are options for snorkelling, surfing and scuba diving. The Galle international cricket stadium in the nearby town regularly features games.
Transport	**Public transport:** Tuk tuks, three wheel taxis and local buses available. **Roads:** From Colombo, take a car/bus/train to Galle. From Galle, if you're on a very low budget then you can get a bus (any going east in the vague direction of Matara) for a few rupees. Best bet is to get a three-wheeler from Galle – about 150 rupees and a 15 minute ride.

Crime rate	As for the country as a whole, there are some risks of terrorism but most trips are trouble-free. The Unawatuna region is trouble-free. While violent crimes against foreigners are relatively infrequent, you should take precautions to safeguard your valuables, especially passports and money.
Main types of employment	Fishing, farming, service and guesthouses.
Future plans	Still yet to be explored and commercially developed, this is due for imminent change when the influx of westerners invest into the beautiful and tranquil beaches of Unawatuna. The government, together with other agencies, is constructing a new highway from Colombo to Matara that will be completed in 2007 and will cut down the journey time to Galle to 1 hour and to Matara to 1 hour 30 minutes.
Yield range	5–7%

Type of property	Entry price	Rent – peak	Rent – off peak	Average annual yield
2 bed apartment	£16,000	£100	£90	7%
3 bed apartment	£27,000	£130	£130	5.7%
3 bed townhouse	£27,000	£130	£130	5.7%
Detached	£31,000	£140	£140	5.4%

Demand for letting	Peak Very high		Off peak Moderately high

Finance and leisure scores	Financial (out of 5) 3	Leisure (out of 5) 4	Total (out of 10) 7

Flights scheduled from	London Airports and other major cities in the UK

Typical cost of flights	Peak £550–1000	Off peak £400–800

Operators	Gulf Air, Srilankan Airlines, Czech Air, Emirates, Qatar Airways, Etihad Airways, British Airways
Description	76 miles south of Colombo, the number one beach destination in Sri Lanka, the sleepy fishing hamlet Unawatuna has a mythical and historical past, which makes it a very special place. Unawatuna is a gorgeous beach, rightly deserving the Discovery Channel's title 'best beach in the world'. Cheap entry prices but finance will be difficult so expect to pay cash for the property. Interest rates are extremely high so it's better, if you can, to borrow in the UK to finance the purchase if you have to. This is a moderately risky investment so if you're a nervous investor then stay away!
Hot website	www.ubr.lk

Estate agents:			
Name	**Address**	**Tel**	**Web**
Lanka Land			www.lankaland.com info@lankaland.com
Overseas Real Estate			overseasrealestate. net/Asia/sri_lanka/
Silver Lanka Land	G&H House, Aluth Wellewe Watte, Mihripenne, Talpe Galle, Sri Lanka	+94 912282356	www.metatrip.com/ lankaland
Lanka Real estate			www.lankareale state.com info@lankarealestate. com
Letting agents:			
Name	**Address**	**Tel**	**Web**
Silver Lanka Land	G&H House, Aluth Wellewe Watte, Mihripenne, Talpe Galle, Sri Lanka	(+94) 912282356	www.metatrip.com/ lankaland

Thailand, Phuket, Pattaya

Country

Population	61.80 million
Population growth	0.930%
Land area	511,770 sq km
Currency and exchange rate	1 baht (B$) = 100 satang (~0.0134312 GBP)
GDP-PPP method	US$387,548.0 millions
GDP growth	0.870%
GDP per head	US$6,271.0 Thousands per person

Financial	Interest rate 2.2%	Inflation rate 2%

National bank	Bank of Thailand
Political	Since the last military coup in May 1992, Thailand has enjoyed almost a decade of rule by democratically elected governments and a far-reaching process of political reform. 1997 saw two watershed events: the economic crisis in July, and the adoption of a new Constitution in October which aimed at improving the selection of political office holders, reducing the scope for corruption and promoting human rights. Implementation of the new provisions has not always lived up to expectations, partly due to the time involved in revising legislation, but the overall impact on Thailand's political landscape has been significant.
Social security	Yes
Languages	Thai, English
Customaries	Present day Thai society is the result of years of cultural mixing, in particular with China and India, yet is being convincingly influenced by the west. Upon meeting a westerner, a handshake is the most formal introduction. A Thai will be greeted with the traditional closed hands and a slight bow of the head, the *wai*. Shoes should be removed when entering a household or temple. Informal attire is widely acceptable and men seldom wear suits. Beachwear should be confined to the beach and topless sunbathing is frowned upon. Smoking is widely acceptable. It is a good idea not to make public displays of anger. Thais regard such behaviour as undisciplined and ill mannered.
Ethnic make-up	Thai 75.0%; Chinese 14.0%; Other 11.0%

Tax	Income Tax			Capital Gains Tax
	Taxable income (baht)		**Tax rate**	Gains derived from sales of real property are subject to Person Income Tax. A standard allowance is deductible, depending on the number of years of ownership. This tax is also applied to gains derived from sales of real property used in trade or business.
	Exceeding (bhat)	**Not exceeding (bhat)**	**%**	
	0	50,000	0	
	50,000	100,000	5	
	100,000	500,000	10	
	500,000	1,000,000	20	
	1,000,000	4,000,000	30	
	4,000,000	–	37	
Description	Thailand's economy was the fastest growing in the world in the 1990s before the Asian financial crisis of 1997. Since then, the economy has made good recovery but has been dampened by the slow pace of economic and structural reform. A significant factor in this slow recovery is the large volume of non-performing loans (NPLs) that have still not been cleared out of the banking system. However, growth is anticipated, fuelled by continuing export growth with increased private and infrastructure investment. The increased confidence in the Thai economy coupled with the weakening of the US dollar, has seen the Baht appreciate almost 10% over 2003. Major industries: services and tourism, manufacturing, vehicles and electronics and agriculture. Major trading partners: the US, Japan, Singapore, Malaysia, China, Hong Kong, Taiwan and the UK. At the time of going to print the Tsunami disaster happened. Property values, as far as we can tell, have not been affected. The real effect will be known around September 2005 to see if holiday bookings have actually reduced. If they do reduce I can see it only being a temporary reduction and prices will bounce back even stronger.			

	Local data

Investor profile	Cash & equity investor; pension investor; holiday investor; retirement investor; downshifter investor; business investor
Category	Bronze

Population	**Total** 200,000	**British** 1,000

Climate	Hours of sunshine per day in summer	Average rainfall per year	Average temperature January	Average temperature July	Average water temperature
	9	The September–October period is the wettest.	24°C	33.4°C	27°C

Proximity to	**Airport:** Phuket International Airport (HKT) is 35km (22 miles) northwest of Phuket.

	Beach: Patong Beach is the main tourist area. Patong also has a beautiful long beach totalling a distance of several kilometres. Bangtao is a large open bay with one of Phuket's longest beaches. Surin Beach is a quiet and very relaxing beach and there are numerous other beaches and islands to explore.
	Nearest city: Many islands surround Phuket and are accessible by boat and road via bridges.
Restaurants and bars	Most bars and pubs are located along or near Bangla Road and Soi Sunset. Phuket Fantasea 'the ultimate cultural theme park' is at Kamala Beach, about 9 km north of Patong. There is a wide range of restaurants available especially within Phuket and neighbouring islands with Thai food being internationally famous. Whether chilli-hot or comparatively bland, harmony is the guiding principle behind each dish.
Sports and leisure facilities	Scuba diving, snorkelling, swimming, wind surfing, sailing, deep-sea fishing, mountain biking, golf, Thai boxing, extreme sports.
Transport	**Public transport:** Daytime bus service to most parts of the island, on a set loop between beach locations. Attempts by the authorities to improve the bus service are opposed by the tuk-tuk (taxi) drivers. Tuk-tuks are now extinct on Phuket and have been replaced with small red vans with open sides. The ubiquitous longtail boat is found wherever there is water in southern Thailand and is also available for hire in Phuket.
	Roads: The natural beauty of the island, and the winding mountain roads, all make Phuket a natural for cruising around, with motorbikes being the most common mode of transportation on the island. Cars and jeeps can be rented at numerous locations.
Crime rate	There are reports of some unlicensed taxis and minibuses overcharging tourists for airport transfers. Airport limousines or licensed taxis with yellow number plates can be hired from the official taxi rank at Bangkok Airport or other international and domestic airports. Be wary of accepting food or drink from strangers – it may be drugged. As with any major tourist destination, be wary of the usual characters and remember to not get involved in local ambiguous dealings as the authorities impose heavy penalties.
Main types of employment	Service industries – food, taxis, entertainment. A huge tourist area with the usual services.
Future plans	To expand on the tourist services and improve connections to other beaches and towns.
Yield range	4–8%

Type of property	Entry price	Rent – peak	Rent – off peak	Average annual yield
2 bed apartment	£22,000	£150	£120	7.36%
3 bed apartment	£35,000	£180	£140	5.48%
3 bed townhouse	£40,000	£180	£140	4.8%
Detached	£48,000	£220	£160	4.75%

Demand for letting	Peak Very high		Off peak High
Finance and leisure scores	Financial (out of 5) 3	Leisure (out of 5) 3	Total (out of 10) 6
Flights scheduled from	London, though connecting services offered from some other major cities.		
Typical cost of flights	Peak £700–1300		Off peak 450–1200
Operators	Thai Airways, Malaysian airlines, British Airways, Air France		
Description	Phuket is located on the west coast, in the southern part of Thailand. This largest island of Thailand, which is surrounded by 32 other islands, has a total area of 570 square kilometres. Phuket is broken by mountains and valleys throughout. The cost of living on this island is very low so a cheap holiday is always to be had. Unfortunately this results in poor yields unless you can sign your property up with a UK agent who can secure you a constant supply of English tenants through the peak season. I was unable to find such an agent but they are out there. If you are seriously thinking of investing in here then source a reliable agent prior to purchase. Capital gains will be high as Thailand always has intrigue.		
Hot website	www.phuketinfo.com		

Estate agents:

Name	Address	Tel	Web
Phuket LandSearch Ltd	Patong, A. Kathu, Phuket 83150	+66 76 340348, 340207	phuketland.com/ villa_santi info@phuketland.com
Blaauw & Nassau Ltd		+66 76 263 737/8	info@blaauw- nassau.com
International Phuket Real Estate	53 Rat-U-Thit Rd Patong Beach, Kathu, Phuket 83150	+ 66 76 344530 1	www.phuket- realestate.com/ info@phuket- realestate-law.com
Brithai Real Estate	9/5 Prachanukroa Road, Patong, Kathu, Phuket 83150	+66 76 076 341608 9	www.phuket- estate.com

Letting agents:

Name	Address	Tel	Web
Blaauw & Nassau Ltd.		+66 76 263 737/8	info@blaauw- nassau.com
International Phuket Real Estate	53 Rat-U-Thit Rd, Patong Beach, Kathu, Phuket 83150	+ 66 76 344530 1	www.phuket- realestate.com/ info@phuket- realestate-law.com

United Arab Emirates, Dubai

Country data		
Population	2.41 million	
Population growth	1.62 percent	
Land area	82,880 sq km	
Currency and exchange rate	1 Emirian dirham (Dh$) = 100 fils (~0.148 GBP)	
GDP-PPP method	US$42,882.0 millions	
GDP growth	3.43%	
GDP per head	US$17,812.0 per person	
Financial	Interest rate 7.74%	Inflation rate 2.8%
National bank	Central Bank of United Arab Emirates	
Political	The 1971 constitution enshrines the system of government of the UAE. It consists of the Federal Supreme Council (the rulers of the seven Emirates), a President and Vice President, council of ministers and other representatives from the states. Relations between the UK and the UAE are generally good. A considerable number of expatriates live in the UAE in addition to a sizeable defence base outside NATO. However, relations with Iran are on a downturn due to disputes concerning rights to certain islands.	
Social security	Yes for nationals. The UAE does not impose social security taxes for expatriates.	
Languages	Arabic; Persian; English; Hindi; Urdu	
Customaries	Islam is the principal religion and 90% of the population are Muslims, although the UAE practises religious and cultural tolerance. There are Christian churches and Hindu temples in Dubai and Sharjah. The Islamic calendar is lunar based so dates of celebrations and festivities change each year. It is discourteous to eat, drink or smoke in front of Muslims in daylight hours during Ramadan. It is polite to accept the refreshments customarily offered to visitors. Expatriate, non-Muslim residents can obtain liquor licences from the local police headquarters enabling them to buy alcohol from special shops. Penalties for drunkenness in public can be quite severe.	
Ethnic make-up	South Asian 50.0%; other Arab and Iranian 23.0%; Emiri 19.0%; other expatriates 8.0%	
Tax	**Income Tax** No personal taxation currently exists in the UAE. Taxes are however imposed on oil and petrochemical companies and branches of foreign banks.	**Capital Gains Tax** Capital gains are not subject to taxation

▶

Description	The most affluent and powerful state in the UAE is Abu Dhabi. The prosperous UAE has one of the highest GNPs in the world. A heavy reliance on hydrocarbons still exists, yet there is much foreign investment and economic diversification. UAE is diversifying the economy into trade, tourism, and heavily subsidized agriculture and high technology industries. Abu Dhabi's internet penetration rate is the highest in the Arab world and exceeds that of a number of EU nations. Ten % of the world's oil reserves lie in the UAE, with Abu Dhabi itself holding 95% of all hydrocarbon deposits and Dubai and Sharjah predominantly sharing the remainder. Dubai is quite different. Due to limited reserves it has had to diversify and create other options to generate local economic benefits. It has a booming tourist industry, increased amounts of flights and is regarded as the hub where east meets west with a significant number of connecting flights going through Dubai. The northern states fare less well and are considerably reliant upon Abu Dhabi and the government.

Local data	
Investor profile	Cash & equity investor; pension investor; downshifter investor; business investor
Category	Gold

Population	Total 872,700	British 35,000

Climate	**Days of sunshine** average 340 a year	**Days of rain per year** Rainfall is infrequent and irregular, mostly during the winter months, but flash floods can occur	**Average temperature January** 10°C/50°F	**Average temperature July** 48°C/118°F	**Average water temperature** 18–32°C

Proximity to	**Airport:** Dubai International Airport, located 5 kilometres southeast of the city centre, is the busiest airport in the Middle East. **Beach:** Burj Al Arab, a unique six-star hotel has great access to beaches. Beautiful beaches between palm island and Dubai Marina. **Nearest city:** Abu Dhabi
Restaurants and bars	Many restaurants in Dubai, from Arabic, Indian and Greek right through to Japanese, Russian, Chinese and Thai. In most Islamic countries, the consumption and retail of alcohol is strictly forbidden. However, in Dubai alcohol is tolerated and you can see foreigners openly guzzling down a pint or two in the city bars. There is no specific nightlife area and most bars are in hotels that are scattered throughout the city. However, cheaper and independent bars can be found within the city too.

	A more relaxed nightly affair is the smoking of tobacco from a shisha pipe in many of the chic coffee houses.
Sports and leisure facilities	Dubai has outstanding sporting and conference facilities and has been declared the number one golf destination worldwide by the International Golf Tour Operators Association. 　Horse riding is available at several riding centres, and rides through the desert are organised regularly. The Dubai world cup has the richest prize of all horse races. 　Boat racing for about 30 rowers is a traditional sport that is becoming increasingly popular. Camel and horse races are also held. Football has become more popular and can be seen in most large towns and there are three thriving rugby clubs in Dubai. Falconry is extremely popular among Arabs.
Transport	**Public transport:** There is no rail system in the UAE. Car hire and chauffeur driven cars are available for hire. Taxis, car hire, airlines and bus all provide a means of travelling to and from the major airport. **Roads:** Much of the road between Abu Dhabi and Dubai is being upgraded. Surfaced roads along the coast link all the emirates.
Crime rate	The UAE as a whole prides itself on a low crime rate and the crime rate in Dubai is decreasing year on year.
Main types of employment	With only roughly 20% of the Dubai economy coming from oil there had been a considerable amount of people employed within the tourism and services industry. The statistics prior to the Iraq war indicated a huge increase of tourism in the idyllic areas surrounding Dubai. However, the war in Iraq has put major strain on the city and its tourist industry. 　Others are mainly employed in manufacturing and trade.
Future plans	The immediate future prospects of the Emirate's tourist industry and its economic situation as a whole seem certain to be governed by developments in the rest of the Middle East. 　Despite the continuing Middle Eastern disruptions the national carrier, Emirates Airlines, plans to increase flights and connections from London and other major western cities. The completion of the new terminal to accommodate this is expected to be complete by 2006.
Yield range	10–15%

Type of property	Entry price	Rent – peak	Rent – off peak	Average annual yield
2 bed apartment	£15,000	£130	£120	10%
3 bed apartment	£18,000	£200	£200	13.3%
3 bed townhouse	£20,000	£240	£240	14.4%
Detached	£23,000	£290	£290	15%

Demand for letting	Peak	Off peak
	Very high	With the beach hotels running at close to 90 % occupancy all year it is still high

Finance and leisure scores	Financial (out of 5) 4	Leisure (out of 5) 5	Total (out of 10) 9
Flights scheduled from	Frequent flights from major cities including London, Birmingham and Manchester		

Typical cost of flights	Peak £250–500	Off peak £170–300

Operators	Emirates, British Airways, Royal Brunei Airlines, Biman Bangladesh, KLM, Lufthansa, Alitalia, Cathay Pacific, Ghana Airways, Gulf Air, Kenya Airways, Kuwait Airways, Malaysia Airlines, Oman Air, Qatar Airways, Turkish Airways and Yemen Airways.
Description	Dubai is the second largest of seven Emirates, and is split into two areas that are divided by the Dubai Creek. The Deira area is around the Dubai international airport and is the more traditional side of Dubai. Bur Dubai is the more modern, cosmopolitan, business area on the other side of the creek. NO TAX! That's the government's policy whether it's income or capital gains. Considering the properties are cheap here as well the likelihood of growth is high. There are lots of off-plan developments for sale here but stay away! There are plenty of re-sale properties that are just as good but half the price. Due to the uncertainty over the war you will be able to pick up a bargain. There are few buyers and if you find someone desperate to sell then bingo! Accept that this hotspot is a risk in the short term but definitely not in the long term.
Hot website	www.dubai-tourist.com

Estate agents:

Name	Address	Tel	Web
Alpha Properties	Al Reem Tower; Office# 1301; Al Maktoum Street; Deira; Dubai PO Box 1038; Dubai	+971 4 2288588	www.alphaproperties. com info@alphaproperties. com
Arenco Real Estate	PO Box 9168, Dubai	+971 4 3372402	ikaar.com/almoosa/ realestate
Union Properties	Union Properties, PO Box 24649, Dubai	+971 4 2046211	http://www.up.ae/ up/ up@unionproperties. com
Colliers International	PO Box 71591, Dubai	+971 4 332 3215	www.colliers.com/ /Markets/UAE/

Letting agents:			
Name	Address	Tel	Web
Union Properties	Union Properties, PO Box 24649, Dubai	+971 4 2046211	http://www.up.ae/up/ up@unionproperties.com
Colliers International	PO Box 71591, Dubai	+971 4 332 3215	www.colliers.com/Markets/UAE/

Europe

Bulgaria, Golden Sands
Croatia, Dubrovnik
Cyprus, Limassol
France, Nimes
Greece, Naxos Island
Malta, Gozo, Sannat
Hungary, Budapest
Ireland, Kinsale, County Donegal
Italy, Isola d'Elba, Tuscany
Poland, Krakow
Portugal, Lagos, Redondo
Spain, Murcia
Turkey, Fethiye

Bulgaria, Golden Sands

Country data

Population	7.71 million
Population growth	−1.140%
Land area	110,550 sq km
Currency and exchange rate	1 lev (Lv) = 100 stotinki (~0.342 GBP)
GDP-PPP method	US$35,820.0 millions
GDP growth	5.20%
GDP per head	US$4,647.0 thousands per person
Financial	**Interest rate** 3.31% · **Inflation rate** 5.80%
National bank	Bulgarian National Bank
Political	Bulgaria is a parliamentary republic ruled by a democratically elected government. Following the collapse of the communist regime, Bulgaria suffered through a series of governments. The elected Bulgarian Socialist Party (BSP) in 1994 were not effective in taking action against corruption and organised crime and making much needed economic reforms. In 1997 the centre−right Union of Democratic forces and a party representing the Turkish minority, Movement for Rights and Freedom, took some seats for the first time. Reforms did take place including membership to NATO and the EU, yet employment levels and standards of living fell, as did the government in 2001. The elections in 2001 were won by former King Simeon II with the National Movement Simeon II (SNM). His simple messages of low taxes, reduced crime, eradication of corruption and higher pensions were of broad appeal. The latest countrywide local elections showed a record low number of voters at 33%.
Social security	Yes
Languages	Bulgarian; various others
Customaries	Usual courtesies should be observed and handshaking is the normal form of greeting. Dress should be conservative but casual. If invited to the home, a small souvenir from one's homeland is an acceptable gift. Do not give money. Remember that a nod of the head means 'No' and a shake means 'Yes'.
Ethnic make-up	Bulgarian 83.0%; Turkish 9.0%; other 6.0%; Roma 3.0%

▶

Tax	Income Tax			Capital Gains Tax
	Taxable income			Inheritance tax is levied on all property in Bulgaria, but no indication of capital gains tax.
		Tax on lower amount	**Rate on excess**	
	Exceeding (BGN)	**Not exceeding (BGN)**	**(BGN)**	**%**	
	0	110	0	0	
	110	140	0	18	
	120	400	5.4	24	
	400	1,000	67.8	28	
	1,000	–	235.8	29	

Description	Bulgaria had a strong agricultural history: main products maize, wheat, sugar, barley, grapes and tobacco. However, it has experienced some decline and major industries are now chemicals, machine building and metalworking, food processing, construction materials and power generation. It is also known for wine and perfumeries. Bulgaria has made significant economic advances but has suffered the usual problems experienced by centrally planned economies adjusting to market conditions. Unemployment is still quite high, around 15%. The key challenges for the government are to attract greater foreign investment, complete the privatisation process, tackle corruption and promote public sector reform.

Local data	
Investor profile	Cash & Equity investor; pension investor; downshifter investor; business investor
Category	Bronze

Population	**Total** 310,000	**British** 1,000

Climate	Hours of sunshine per day in summer	Average rainfall per year	Average temperature January	Average temperature July	Average water temperature
	10	35 days	8°C	26°C	21°C

Proximity to	Airport: 17 km **Beach:** Golden Sands, called the seaside capital of Bulgaria **Nearest city:** Dobrich
Restaurants and bars	Numerous lively discos and bars, a variety of folk taverns and restaurants. Many restaurants are cheap, good and offer friendly service in addition to English menus!

	There are hundreds of places to go for a night out. Bulgaria and Varna have an Italian style café culture. Davidoff cafés are an institution. Large numbers of live music venues are usually tucked away in basements.
Sports and leisure facilities	Tennis courts, mini golf, horse riding, jet skis, paragliding, sailing and motor boats, windsurfing, yacht club, water-skiing, banana rides, cycling, bowling and diving
Transport	**Public transport:** Good links around the city and regular bus services to beach resorts. Cheap taxis available on the streets.
	Roads: The roads offer good links to other cities throughout Bulgaria.
Crime rate	Low, but be on guard for the usual pickpockets at a tourist destination.
Main types of employment	Mainly tourism and service. Varna is one of the biggest science centres in Bulgaria and there are five institutions of higher education in Varna. Varna is also involved in busy shipping, shipbuilding and ship repairing activities.
Future plans	Challenge Sofia and Plovdiv as the third biggest city.
Yield range	7–10%

Types of property	Entry price	Rent – peak	Rent – off peak	Average annual yield
2 bed apartment	£11,000	£110	£70	9.8%
3 bed apartment	£20,000	£160	£140	9%
3 bed townhouse	£21,000	£180	£130	8.5%
Detached	£26,000	£220	£130	7.3%

Demand for letting	Peak		Off peak	
	Fairly high		Moderate	

Finance and leisure scores	**Financial** (out of 5)	**Leisure** (out of 5)	**Total** (out of 10)
	3	3	6

Flights scheduled from	London, Bradford, Glasgow, Leeds	

Typical costs of flights	Peak	Off peak
	£400	£169–200

Operators	British Airways, Hemus Air, Malev Airways, Britannia, Thomson, Bulgaria Air, Balkan Holidays Air
Description	Apart from being a beach resort, Varna rivals Sofia and Plovdiv in cultural attractions and historic buildings, museums and art galleries. It also provides access to some of the quieter scenic spots along the coast, including the nature reserve of Kamchiya, the royal palace of Balchik and the hillside monastery of Aladzha.

▶

	What I like about this area is the only way is up! You can enter buy with a little bit more than a few grand, get okay yields and if it all goes belly up you haven't broken the bank. I expect that the capital gains will be spectacular as this area is being talked up a lot. Whether the gains are genuine or all hype is unsure. I would set yourself an exit target of doubling your money: if you buy something for £20,000 then sell at £40,000. If this doesn't happen in three years then sell anyway as long as you do not realise a loss. Political stability is increasing but you could find yourself owning an idyllic property in the middle of a potential war zone! Be cautious.
Hot website	http://www.bulgaria.com/varna/

Estate agents:

Name	Address	Tel	Web
DAO Real Estate		+359 52 603 731	daoreal@daoreal.com www.daoreal.com/
Golden Eye Real Estate	Knyaz Boris I No 28; Floor 1; Varna 9000; Bulgaria	+359 (0)52 641856	goldeneye@tcinbg.net http://goldeneye. tcinbg.net/
Kirov	Bulgaria, 9000 Varna, Maria Louisa Bld. 28	+359 52 610 39(1-4)	http://www.kirov.bg/

Letting agents:

Name	Address	Tel	Web
Golden Eye Real Estate	Knyaz Boris I No 28; Floor 1; Varna 9000; Bulgaria	+359 (0)52 641856	goldeneye@tcinbg.net http://goldeneye. tcinbg.net/
Kirov	Bulgaria, Varna 9000, Maria Louisa, Bld. 28	+359 52 610 39(1–4)	http://www.kirov.bg/

Croatia, Dubrovnik

Country data		
Population	4.33 million	
Population growth	1.21%	
Land area	56,410 sq km	
Currency and exchange rate	1 Croatian kuna (HRK) = 100 lipas (~0.0901978 GBP)	
GDP-PPP method	US$24,158.0 millions	
GDP growth	2.85%	
GDP per head	US$5,574.0 thousands per person	
Financial	Interest rate 4.5%	Inflation rate 2.2%
National bank	Croatian National Bank	
Political	Legislative power rests with the bicameral Sabor, both houses of which are directly elected. Executive power is held by the President, who appoints a cabinet of ministers. Before President Tudjman's death in 1999 the failure to meet international commitments to human rights and democratic standards isolated Croatia from the European mainstream. Since Tudjman's death, much has changed. Recent governments have acted positively on initiatives to tackle the problems of displaced refugees, restructuring the Croatian national army and civil service and constitutional reform. Croatia was recently accepted into the NATO Membership Action Plan (MAP), and is now working to implement the Stabilisation and Association Agreement (SAA) which it signed with the EU last year. Relations with Croatia's neighbours, particularly Serbia and Montenegro and Bosnia-Herzegovina, have improved significantly.	
Social security	Yes	
Languages	Croatian; Italian; Hungarian; Czech; Slovak; Slovenian and German. Istriot, Istro-Romanian and Serbo-Croatian also have been spoken in specific regions or at specific points in recent history.	
Customaries	People normally shake hands upon meeting and leaving. Smoking is generally acceptable but there are restrictions in public buildings and on public transport. Certain restrictions exist on taking photographs.	
Ethnic make-up	Croat 78.1%; Serb 12.2%; other 6.6%; Bosniak .9%; Hungarian .5%; Slovenian .5%; Czech .4%; Albanian .3%; Roma.2%;	

▶

Tax	Income Tax			Capital Gains Tax
	Taxable income		Rate on excess	Capital gains derived from the sale of a property or real estate are not taxed, with the exception of capital gains derived from real estate held for less than three years and not used by the owner or dependent family members for lodging.
	Exceeding (HRK)	Not exceeding (HRK)	%	
	0	30,000	15	
	30,000	75,000	25	
	75,000	–	35	
Description	After the effects of war and financial mismanagement, the Racan government tried to stabilise public finances. With substantial support and investment from abroad, the economy has recovered moderately well. The government introduced budget cuts and started a broad economic reform programme. Major industries include steel, cement, chemicals, fertilisers, textiles and pharmaceuticals. The main trading partners are the EU, Slovenia, and Bosnia and Herzegovina. The economy is slowly growing yet more reforms are required to reduce the 23% official unemployment rate. Priority areas include pensions, health and the ending of subsidies. The Dalmatian Coast is a key area for tourism and, after the ravages of the war, the beach and sunshine provide a healthy outlook for future tourist initiatives.			
Local data				
Investor profile	Cash & equity Investor; pension investor; downshifter investor; business investor			
Category	Bronze			
Population	Total 125,000		British 800	

Climate	Hours of sunshine per day in summer	Average rainfall per year	Average temperature January	Average temperature July	Average water temperature
	11	24 days	14°C	29°C	20°C

Proximity to	**Airport:** 20 km from the city of Dubrovnik **Beach:** Beaches are lined all along the Adriatic coast **Nearest city:** Ploce
Restaurants and bars	In the old town there are loads of good pizzerias in little side streets and squares. Many restaurant touts can be found along the Placa but they are harmless and most are really friendly.

	The main street of the old core of the town is the Placa. It is a non-traffic area, as is the rest of the old historic centre of the town. Many of those who have visited the town comment that this is one of the most beautiful streets in the whole world. There are many bars and pubs with great offers to tempt you in. There are also many Irish bars.
Sports and leisure facilities	Boating and sailing. Some people come to Croatia just to sail in the Adriatic Sea. One look at the glistening blue water and the beautiful coastline will tell you why. Other popular activities are fishing, scuba diving, parachuting and basketball. Football is a passion in Dubrovnik although not to the degree that the locals in Split and Zagreb are nutty about their respective teams!
Transport	**Public Transport:** The main bus station is located about 3 km outside of the old town next to the port in the suburb called Gruz. Dubrovnik is well serviced by bus from all over the country and there is a local bus station right across the street from the station. **Roads:** It can also be reached by bus from Zagreb (which takes about 12 hours), Rijeka, Split or Trieste in Italy. The most pleasant journey to the city is probably by ferry from Rijeka, which stops at many islands and ports along the way, and takes about 17 hours. There are also international ferry services from Bari and Ortona, near Pescara (only in summer), in Italy.
Crime rate	It is quite safe to travel all over Croatia and mugging and thefts are not a problem. You can safely walk in any town at night, but use your common sense, as always.
Main types of employment	Services, tourism and agriculture
Future plans	To provide passengers with the highest quality and widest range of services, in line with other international airports. Major development works are being undertaken for a new, modern identity for Dubrovnik Airport for the 21st century. It will have a capacity of 2 million passengers a year.
Yield range	4–10%

Type of property	Entry price	Rent – peak	Rent – off peak	Average annual yield
2 bed apartment	£30,000	£300	£180	9.6%
3 bed apartment	£40,000	£500	£200	9.6%
3 bed townhouse	£65,000	£400	£200	5.5%
Detached	£75,000	£400	£200	4.8%

Demand for letting	Peak Very high		Off peak Moderate	

Finance and leisure scores	Financial (out of 5) 3	Leisure (out of 5) 3	Total (out of 10) 6

▶

Flights scheduled from	Gatwick, Heathrow, Manchester fly directly to Dubrovnik. There are also some cheaper flights from London Stansted.		
Typical cost of flights	**Peak** £200–300		**Off peak** £130–200
Operators	British Airways, Croatian Airways, Sky Europe, Germanwings, Alitialia, Austrian Airlines		

Description	Dubrovnik's beauty has always attracted and fascinated people. With its 17 monasteries and churches and one of the oldest synagogues in Europe, it is a cultural heritage monument and protected by UNESCO.
	    It is another place that has been talked up a lot and is yet to deliver. Again I would tread with caution. Property prices are low but so are rental prices. There is a lot of hype surrounding this area so you can bank upon capital growth as your main income earner. Sell within three years and then see what the market does.
	    Interest rates and inflation rates are comparable to ours but do not let that mask the political uncertainty of the country. Get in now, if this is a pet favourite of yours, because the prices are low, but do not invest your life savings as a lot can change.		

Hot website	www.visit-croatia.co.uk/dubrovnik/		

Estate agents:

Name	Address	Tel	Web
Dream Property Croatia	Nikole Tesle 4, 20000 Dubrovnik, Croatia,	+385 (0) 20 435535	www.dreamcroatia. com
Optic Cruise World Ltd	Put Tihe 4a, Cavtat/Dubrovnik, 20210	+385 91 523 4806	http://dubrovnikreal estate.turbonet.com
Dubrovnik Real Estate	Andrije Hebranga, 53, 20000, Dubrovnik, Croatia	+385 (0) 91 504 20 20	www.dubrovnik-area.com/real-estate real-estate@post. hinet.hr

Letting agents:

Name	Address	Tel	Web
Dubrovnik Real Estate	Andrije Hebranga, 53, 20000, Dubrovnik, Croatia	+385 (0) 91 504 20 20	www.dubrovnik-area.com/real-estate real-estate@post. hinet.hr

Cyprus, Limassol

Country data

Population	920,600
Population growth	0.56%
Land area	9,240 km²
Currency and exchange rate	1 CYP = 1.14232 GBP
GDP-PPP method	–
GDP growth	2.00%
GDP per head	$13,900

Financial	Interest rate 5%	Inflation rate 2.8%

National Bank	Central Bank of Cyprus

Political	The 1960 constitution, which allowed for a population-determined sharing of power between the Turkish and Greek communities, officially remains in force. However, in practice, the state organs that it established are duplicated in the two zones.
	    Cyprus has been divided since 1974 when Turkish troops invaded the northern part of the island. Thus the Republic of Cyprus remains generally the Greek Cypriot part of the country. The northern part of the island refers to itself as the Turkish Republic of Northern Cyprus (TRNC), but is not internationally recognised. In May 2004 Greek Cyprus joined the European Union. Yet Cyprus remained divided. Politics on both sides of the island are dominated by the continued division of Cyprus. There have been several initiatives since 1974 to try to achieve a settlement all of which have run into the sand.
	    The executive President is elected for a five-year term, and exercises executive power through a Council of Ministers appointed by him.

Social security	Yes
Languages	Greek, Turkish, English
Customaries	Respect should be shown for religious beliefs. It is customary to shake hands and other normal courtesies should be observed. It is viewed as impolite to refuse an offer of Greek coffee or a cold drink. Beachwear should be confined to the beach or poolside. Between 1300–1600 hours is siesta time in the summer (May–September). Photography is forbidden near military camps or installations.
Ethnic make-up	Greek 85.0%; Turkish 12.0%; Other 3.0%

Tax	Income Tax			Capital Gains Tax
	Taxable income (£)	Tax on lower amount	Rate on excess	Tax at a rate of 20% is levied on gains from all immovable property located in Cyprus.
	Exceeding (£) / Not exceeding (£)	(£)	%	
	0 — 9,000	0	0	
	9,000 — 12,000	0	20	
	12,000 — 15,000	600	25	
	15,000 — –	1,350	30	
	Spouses are taxed separately, not jointly, on all types of income.			

Description	The economy remains export-orientated with manufactured goods. The southern Greek-Cypriot region has a strong agricultural sector, producing fruit, vegetables, barley, citrus and grapes. Major trading partners: the US, UK, Italy, Greece, Russia, Bulgaria and Germany. Since 1996 the negative economic trend has been dampened and reversed. Tourism is the main component to GDP growth. The growing importance of the services industry and also the growing offshore financial services is also a major contributor. The northern Turkish controlled region has been severely limited in economic growth and relies quite heavily on Turkish subsidies.

Local data

Investor profile	Cash & equity investor; pension investor; holiday investor; retirement investor; downshifter investor
Category	Bronze

Population	Total 150,000	British 10,000

Climate	Hours of sunshine per day in summer	Average rainfall per year	Average temperature January	Average temperature July	Average water temperature
	10	10 days	19°C	30°C	23°C

Proximity to	**Airport:** 45 minutes to Larnaca airport **Beach:** Ladies Mile **Nearest city:** Pafos

Restaurants and bars	You will find many bars, restaurants and clubs. The old town of Limassol in the area around the castle contains lots of funky bars and coffee shops where many Cypriots hang out. Limassol has a bright and lively nightlife, along with some of the best festivals on the Island: eg the wine festival in September.

	Plenty of restaurants line the beach all offering competitive prices. Walking around Limassol you will find restaurants of all kinds.
Sports and leisure facilities	Water sports, diving, tennis, gymnasiums, aerobics classes and aqua classes. Limassol also boasts water parks.
Transport	**Public transport:** There is public transport service with regular connections between cities, with scheduled taxi services and comfortable coaches. Private taxis and rental cars are readily available.
	Roads: Distances between towns are relatively short, covered by a good network of modern roads. The short distances between cities are becoming even shorter due to a motorway network, which is constantly being extended and upgraded.
Crime rate	Remarkably low
Main types of employment	Cyprus has a major winemaking industry, and an important commercial and tourist centre.
Future plans	To improve its tourist attractions and become further integrated into the Eurozone.
Yield range	6–9%

Type of property	Entry price	Rent – peak	Rent – off peak	Average annual yield
2 bed apartment	£60,000	£340	£300	6.4%
3 bed apartment	£76,000	£570	£480	8.2%
3 bed townhouse	£80,000	£550	£450	7.5%
Detached	£100,000	£600	£600	7.2%

Demand for letting	Peak		Off peak	
	Very high		High	

Finance and leisure scores	Financial (out of 5)	Leisure (out of 5)	Total (out of 10)
	3	3	6

Flights scheduled from	Heathrow, Gatwick, Manchester, Newcastle, Bristol, Southampton, Birmingham, Glasgow

Typical cost of flights	Peak	Off peak
	£130–210	£80–150

Operators	British Airways, Cyprus Airways, SN Brussels, Helios Airways, Olympic Airways, Air 2000, charter flights
Description	Limassol is the second largest town in Cyprus. It has a large port busy with ships from all over the world. It's cheap to get to and a lot cheaper to buy than Spain. In fact Cyprus is the new Spain! This part of Cyprus is getting talked up a lot. Even if it is hype buy now and cash in later. There is still room for prices to grow. The climate is comparable to Spain but with half the price tag!
	Yields are not bad but they will grow. Demand is rising due to sophisticated holiday makers requiring an alternative to Spain so rental values will grow thus bettering the yield if you get in now. Expect entry prices above to double in the next five years.

▶

Hot website	http://kypros.org/Cyprus/limassol.html		
Estate agents:			
Name	**Address**	**Tel**	**Web**
Buy Sell Cyprus	Shops 5-6, Posidonos Ave, Myra Court, Kato Paphos, Cyprus	+357 26819012	www.buysellcyprus.com katopaphos@ buysellcyprus.com
CyprusHomes.Org	c/o InterLink Marketing Systems, Highstone House, 165 High Street, Barnet, Herts EN5 5SU, UK	020 8440 9933	info@cyprushomes.org www.cyprushomes.org
Capital Growth Real Estates	Capital Growth Real Estate Agents Ltd, Shop 14, Frixos Business Center, 33 Arch. Makarios Ave III, 6017 Larnaca, Cyprus	+357 24817711	lim@cgestates.com www.cgestates.com
Cyprus Homes	Evangelestrias 65, Kato polemidia, Limassol 4156, Cyprus	+357 25381213	sales@cyprus homes.com.cy www.cyprus homes.com.cy
Letting agents:			
Name	**Address**	**Tel**	**Web**
CyprusHomes.Org	c/o InterLink Marketing Systems, Highstone House, 165 High Street, Barnet, Herts EN5 5SU, UK	020 8440 9933	info@cyprushomes.org www.cyprushomes.org
Capital Growth Real Estates	Capital Growth Real Estate Agents Ltd, Shop 14, Frixos Business Center, 33 Arch. Makarios Ave III, 6017 Larnaca, Cyprus	+357 24817711	lim@cgestates.com www.cgestates.com

France, Nimes		
Country data		
Population	59.55 million	
Population growth	0.370%	
Land area	545,630 sq km	
Currency and exchange rate	1 Euro = 100 cents (~0.664 GBP)	
GDP-PPP method	US$1,363,697.0 millions	
GDP growth	1.42%	
GDP per head	US$22,900.0 per person	
Financial	Interest rate 2%	Inflation rate 1.9%
National bank	Banque de France	
Political	France is a major power in the Eurozone and President Jacques Chirac benefited from its anti-war stance on Iraq, enjoyed high approval ratings – in excess of 80% – from a populace largely opposed to the war. However, it will play a committed part in the rebuilding of Iraq. Local elections in March 2004 gave a profound hammering to Chirac's coalition. The Socialists and other allied parties won 50% of the votes cast and 20 of the 22 regions. The result was a blow to Chirac because it reflected popular discontent regarding the country's unemployment rate and economic woes and he will have to make amends on public reform to win back popularity before the 2007 presidential elections.	
Social security	Yes	
Languages	French	
Customaries	In France, handshaking and kissing of both cheeks are the usual forms of greeting. Meal times are often long and take a leisurely approach, with most offices traditionally taking lunch breaks for up to two hours. Smoking is prohibited in public transport, cinemas and theatres. Visitors should carry some sort of identification such as EU driving licence or passport as spot checks are not uncommon and it is a requirement by law to carry identification.	
Ethnic make-up	Celtic, Latin, Teutonic, Slavic, North African, Indochinese and Basque minorities	

▶

Tax	Income Tax	Capital Gains Tax
	Taxpayers are categorised as residents or non-residents. Non-residents are taxed on French-source income only. The following table presents income tax for the year 2002:	Capital gains derived from the disposal of real estate and shareholdings are subject to tax.

Taxable income (€)		Tax rate
Exceeding (€)	Not exceeding (€)	%
0	4,191	0
4,191	8,242	7.05
8,242	14,506	19.74
14,506	23,489	29.14
23,489	38,218	38.54
38,218	47,131	43.94
47,131	–	49.58

A flat 'social tax' of 8% is imposed on 95% of gross salary.

Non-residents are subject to a withholding tax on French-source compensation, after the deduction of social tax and the 10% and 20% standard deductions.

Gains derived from the disposal of real property held for two years or less are taxed as ordinary income. Gains for property held for two years or more are calculated as the difference between sales price and the inflation-adjusted purchase price, which is then reduced by 5% for each year. Further constraints apply; investigate further for more information. Some exemptions may apply. Also note that a standard deduction of €915 applies to total taxable gains in computing the applicable tax.

Taxable income (€)		Tax rate
Exceeding (€)	Not exceeding (€)	%
0	9,839	0
9,839	28,548	15
28,548	–	25

Tax brackets are prorated according to actual time worked in France.

Description	France has the fourth largest economy in the world after the USA, Japan and Germany. It has a mixed economy with large agricultural, industrial and service sectors. The GDP is dominated by the services sector, followed by industry. Major industries: aerospace, automotive, pharmaceuticals, industrial machinery, food and drink and tourism. Major trading partners; the EU (especially Germany, the UK, Spain, Italy and Belgium) and the USA.
	The government has traditionally played an active role in the French economy, but the recent years of privatisation have slowly dissipated this involvement.

▶

	The French economy has not been immune to the economic slowdown of the last few years and has been sluggish over the last three years and also suffers from a relatively high unemployment rate.
	Local data
Investor profile	Cash & equity investor; pension investor; holiday investor; retirement investor; downshifter investor; business investor;
Category	Gold

Population	Total	British
	130,000	300

Climate	Hours of sunshine per day in summer	Average rainfall per year	Average temperature January	Average temperature July	Average water temperature
	10	45 days	11°C	29°C	19°C

Proximity to	**Airport:** Nimes Airport caters for low-budget airlines and is about 12km out of town. Speed shuttles and taxis are available.
	Beach: You can drive or take a bus a few km south to find spectacular beaches.
	Nearest city: Avignon (or Montpellier)
Restaurants and bars	Plenty of cafés, with the intimacy of the surroundings providing a refreshing atmosphere. Locals veer away from the centre of town to smaller, cosier cafés that are not as expensive. Nimes is not renowned for its frenetic nightlife, but there are many bars and cafés that are open quite late.
Sports and leisure facilities	Many places to go fishing, swimming and canoeing and an hour away on the coast are beaches with water sport facilities, jet-ski or windsurfing. Collias is a good place for rock climbing, as is Saynes.
Transport	**Public transport:** Transport in Nimes is quite good, with all local buses stopping outside the train station. Single ride costs €1, and there are detailed maps showing the bus routes at every stop. There are also buses to the airport. Trains from Nimes to places all over France and the rest of mainland Europe, with direct trains to Marseille, Lyon, Toulouse and many other destinations.
	Roads: The roads provide good access to Montpellier, Perpignan, Avignon, Toulouse and areas further north.
Crime rate	Low
Main types of employment	Nimes has traditionally been dominated by a successful textile manufacturing industry. Nimes Airport is at the centre of much of the new economic activity in the area.
Future plans	The town's rapid expansion is pushing its boundaries further south. The Allées Jean Jaurès are a continuation from the Jardins de la Fontaine and have recently opened out onto the plains to the south by crossing under the railway viaduct.

Yield range	12–15%			
Type of property	Entry price	Rent – peak	Rent – off peak	Average annual yield
2 bed apartment	£45,000	£600	£400	13%
3 bed apartment	£55,000	£800	£700	15.2%
3 bed townhouse	£74,000	£900	£700	12.9%
Detached	£80,000	£1100	£800	13.5%

Demand for letting	Peak		Off peak	
	High		Quite high	

Finance and leisure scores	Financial (out of 5)	Leisure (out of 5)	Total (out of 10)
	5	4	9

Flights scheduled from	London Stansted, Manchester

Typical cost of flights	Peak	Off peak
	£60–80	£40–65

Operators	Air France, Ryanair and some other smaller airlines. Also possible to fly to Paris Charles de Gaulle and take a domestic flight.

Description	Nimes is set against the foothills of the Cévennes and is ideally located for exploring much of the south of France. Nimes boast some fine beaches and the Languedoc Roussillon region combines all the beauty of the sea, country and mountains in addition to the historic treasures and vineyards at the nearby Rhone valley. An inviting and relaxing ambience. Cheap entry prices, fantastic yields, low crime rates – what more do you want? It's cheap to get to with regular flights from Stansted and Manchester or driveable within a day. Investing in France is a sure bet. The country itself is an economic heavyweight and investing in the southern part is even more of one.

Hot website	http://www.ot-nimes.fr/english/

Estate agents:

Name	Address	Tel	Web
French Real Estate	The Pool House, Bicester Road, Stratton Audley, Oxon OX27 9BS	+44 (0)1869 277677	www.frenchinvestment property.com info@frenchinvestment property.com
Fourgassié Immobilier	9 Rue Victor Hugo, 81200 – Mazamet, South France	05 63 98 85 01	
Agence Vitani	3 Rue Théron, 81200 – Mazamet,	05 63 98 88 75	
IMMO' Sud Estate Agency	Sandrine Calvet, Place des Couverts, 09500 Mirepoix	33 (0)561 682.649	www.immo-sud.com/ immo-sud- calvet@wanadoo.fr

Letting agents:			
Name	**Address**	**Tel**	**Web**
IMMO' Sud Estate Agency	Sandrine Calvet, Place des Couverts, 09500 Mirepoix	33 (0)561 682.649	www.immo-sud.com/ immo-sud-calvet@ wanadoo.fr
French Real Estate	The Pool House, Bicester Road, Stratton, Audley, Oxon OX27 9BS	+44 (0)1869 277677	www.frenchinvestment property.com info@frenchinvestment property.com

Greece, Naxos Island

Country data

Population	10.62 million
Population growth	0.210 %
Land area	130,800 sq km
Currency and exchange rate	1 Euro = 100 cents (~0.644 GBP)
GDP-PPP method	US$151,392.0 millions
GDP growth	3.88 %
GDP per head	US$14,250.0 thousands per person
Financial	Interest rate 2% / Inflation rate 3.9%
National bank	Bank of Greece
Political	Greece is a unicameral parliamentary democracy. Executive power rests with the 300-member parliament. The centre-right New Democracy party won office in 2004 for the first time since 1993. Greece joined NATO in 1952 and the EC (now the EU) in 1981.
Social security	Yes
Languages	Greek; some speakers of English, French, Turkish, Macedonian, Romanian, Romani, Bulgarian and Albanian
Customaries	The Greeks have a very strong sense of cultural and historical heritage, and a sense of unity prevails. The Greek Orthodox church plays a strong part in the Greek way of life, especially in the countryside. Greek bureaucracy is very slow. Persistence and attendance in person at the office or ministry concerned is almost the only way of getting things done. Identification documents and various authorisation letters or seals are necessary. Smoking is prohibited on public transport and in public buildings. Taking photographs of military installations is an offence and can be dealt with harshly.
Ethnic make-up	Greek 98.0%; other 2.0%

Tax	Income Tax			Capital Gains Tax
	Taxable income (€)	Tax on lower amount	Rate on excess	Capital gains derived by individuals are generally not taxed.
	Exceeding (€) / Not exceeding (€)	(€)	%	
	0 — 7,400	0	0	
	7,400 — 8,400	0	5	
	8,400 — 13,400	50	15	
	13,400 — 23,400	800	30	
	23,400 —	3800	40	
	Non-residents are taxed on their income at the same rate as residents.			
Description	Tourism is the most important service industry with roughly 10 million visitors per year. Much work on improving the infrastructure and transport network was undertaken prior to the Olympic Games. It is hoped that such improvements will further improve tourism in Greece. Traditionally an agricultural producer, accession to the EU stimulated growth in other areas. Despite the mixed economy with heavy dependence on tourism and shipping, approximately 20% of the labour force still works in agriculture and farming. Major trading partners: European countries, mainly Germany, Italy, France and the UK. It adopted the Euro in 2002.			

Local data				
Investor profile	Cash & equity investor; pension investor; holiday investor; retirement investor; downshifter investor; business investor			
Category	Silver			
Population	Total 18,000		British 100	
Climate	Hours of sunshine per day in summer / Average rainfall per year / Average temperature January / Average temperature July / Average water temperature			
	13 — 15 days — 15°C — 26°C — 22°C			
Proximity to	**Airport:** Olympic Airways links Athens with Naxos and the airport is near Ayios Prokopios **Beach:** Ayia Anna and Plaka **Nearest city:** Paros Island			
Restaurants and bars	The main party scene is in the centre Chora, where there are discos, bars, piano bars and nightclubs with Greek popular music. There are eating-places of all kinds: the typically Greek restaurants (*estiatoria*), serving mostly made-up dishes, tavernas which specialise in grilled meats, souvlaki shops, and seaside restaurants that serve fresh fish. One should try the local specialities, such as wild rabbit or partridge.			

▶

Sports and leisure facilities	Snorkelling, water sports, jet skiing, windsurfing, boating, diving, trekking
Transport	**Public transport:** The island can be reached by air from Athens and by ferry from Piraeus and Rafina. Some ferry services go direct to the island and others make stops at Paros, Ios, Santorini and Tinos. Naxos has a good bus system that lets you easily get to the beaches and villages. **Roads:** Cars, bicycles and motorbikes can be hired.
Crime rate	Low
Main types of employment	Tourism and services
Future plans	To maintain the natural beauty of the island whilst improving its tourism industry.
Yield range	11–16%

Type of property	Entry price	Rent – peak	Rent – off peak	Average annual yield
2 bed apartment	£55,000	£800	£700	16%
3 bed apartment	£64,000	£900	£800	16%
3 bed townhouse	£93,000	£1050	£800	11.6%
Detached	£100,000	£1100	£800	11.4%

Demand for letting	Peak Very high		Off peak High

Finance and leisure scores	Financial (out of 5) 4	Leisure (out of 5) 3	Total (out of 10) 7

Flights scheduled from	London Gatwick, London Luton, Manchester and other major and regional airports (a connecting flight may be required to Naxos)

Typical cost of flights	Peak £120–200	Off peak £80–160

Operators	Easyjet, Malev, Air France, Greek Airways, British Airways, Lufthansa, Czech Airways, Alitalia
Description	Being the largest island in the Cyclades, Naxos has a commodity many of its more illustrious neighbours lack–space. Mountains, lush valleys of citrus and olive groves, pastel-coloured coastal plains and wide stretches of empty, golden sand all but envelop the tiny, quaint villages. You get a great yield and no capital gains tax to pay when you sell. How much capital gain you'll get over time is unsure. This is why I have only given it a silver rating. Even though the area is very pretty and would make a great holiday home, demand for owning property on the island is low. However, there are few properties for sale and the entry level is greater than £55,000. Stick to popular areas and forget any more than 250m from the beach.
Hot website	http://www.naxosnet.com/

Estate agents:			
Name	Address	Tel	Web
Neon Naxos Realty	Platia Protodikiou, Naxos, Cyclades 84300	(011) 0030 285 26644	www.naxosrealty.com kthma@nax.forthnet.gr
Veronis Real Estate	Naxos Island, Cyclades	+30 22850 29211	www.veronis.gr/who/ info@veronis.gr
Takis Kontopoulos, Konstantinos Kapiris	Chora Naxos, Naxos 84300	+30 (2)2850 23157	www.naxos-houses.com/ info@naxos-houses.com
Greek-Estate Ltd	75 Galinou str 187.58, Attica	+30 210 4323198	http://www.sitia.biz/
Letting agents:			
Name	Address	Tel	Web
Neon Naxos Realty	Platia Protodikiou, Naxos, Cyclades 84300	(011) 0030 285 26644	www.naxosrealty.com kthma@nax.forthnet.gr
Veronis Real Estate	Naxos Island, Cyclades	+30 22850 29211	www.veronis.gr/who/ info@veronis.gr

Malta, Gozo, Sannat

Country data	
Population	0.395 million
Population growth	0.740%
Land area	320 sq km
Currency and exchange rate	1 Maltese lira (LM) = 100 cents (~1.559 GBP)
GDP-PPP method	US$5,380.0 millions
GDP growth	−1.730%
GDP per head	US$13,636.0 thousands per person
Financial	Interest rate 3.75% Inflation rate 2.2%
National bank	Central Bank of Malta
Political	Malta's presidency is largely a ceremonial post, whilst executive power is held by the Cabinet. Although the country has enjoyed close links with the UK for 200 years, in recent years close ties with North Africa, notably Libya, contributed towards political division over the question of joining the EU. A referendum in 2003 voted in favour of entry to Europe. Malta shares close trade relations with the EU, which accounts for 46% of Malta's exports and 67% of Malta's total imports (*Central Bank of Malta Quarterly Review* − March 2003).
Social security	Yes
Languages	Maltese, English
Customaries	The usual European courtesies are expected, but the visitor should also bear in mind the tremendous importance of Roman Catholicism; if visiting a church, for instance, modest dress covering the shoulders and legs will be expected. Smoking is prohibited on public transport and in some public buildings, including cinemas.
Ethnic make-up	Maltese

Tax	Income Tax			Capital Gains Tax
	Residents are taxed differently depending on whether or not they are married. Non-residents are taxed on the same level regardless of whether or not they are married.			Taxable capital gains are included with other earnings that are taxed at the rates set forth in income tax rates.
	Taxable income		Tax on lower amount	Rate on excess
	Exceeding (Lm)	Not exceeding (Lm)	(Lm)	%
	0	300	0	0
	300	1,300	0	20
	1,300	3,300	200	30
	3,300	–	800	35

Description	With a small agricultural sector, the tourism and marine support services are two key growth sectors. In addition, although Malta is an island, the fishing sector is relatively insignificant. Approximately 25% of Malta's foreign exchange earnings come through tourism. The industrial sector consists of textiles, clothing, shoes, plastics, printing and electronics.
	The major trading partners are the UK, USA, Italy, France and the Benelux countries. Malta has traditionally enjoyed low unemployment, low inflation and consistent growth rates. The economy is, however, slowing and Malta's large budget deficits and high public debt to GDP ratio are major concerns.
	The government is implementing privatisation, pension reform and tax collection programmes designed to alleviate macroeconomic imbalances.
	Numerous tourist developments are underway in Malta, aimed at revitalizing a sector that has been stagnant for a number of years. Particular emphasis is being placed upon attracting the more affluent traveller.

Local data

Investor profile	Cash & equity investor; pension investor; holiday investor; retirement investor; downshifter investor; business investor
Category	Silver

Population	Total 28,000	British 400

Climate	Hours of sunshine per day in summer	Average rainfall per year	Average temperature January	Average temperature July	Average water temperature
	10	30 days	16°C	25°C	20°C

▶

Proximity to	**Airport:** After reaching Malta by plane, Gozo could be reached either by ferry or by helicopter. From the Malta International Airport, there is a helicopter service operating between the airport and the Gozo Heliport and vice-versa.
	Beach: The crystal clear waters of Marsalforn and Xlendi bays are too beautiful to miss.
	Nearest city: Ta Cenc
Restaurants and bars	You will find many good-priced and expensive restaurants in Gozo. Just pick any restaurant, table by the sea, dining next to the lovely blue water, with the air heavy with the smell of sea spray. Many specialise in fresh fish, fillets steaks, veal, chicken and pasta dishes. You will find mainly family orientated restaurants and drinking establishments. If you want vibrant nightlife and shopping centres then Gozo is not going to be right for you.
Sports and leisure facilities	Diving is one of the most popular activities on the island and attracts divers from around the world. There is swimming, and leisurely walks amongst beautiful scenery.
Transport	**Public transport:** There are some regular bus services from the capital, Victoria, to all towns and villages in Gozo. Taxis are available at Victoria and Mgarr to reach other villages.
	Roads: There are some car, bike and motorbike hire companies available to use the good roads.
Crime rate	Very low to non-existent
Main types of employment	Being an island, the fishing industry has been the main employer for centuries. Farming is also a key employer.
Future plans	To maintain its tranquillity and beauty whilst encouraging investment.
Yield range	12–17%

Type of property	Entry price	Rent – peak	Rent – off peak	Average annual yield
2 bed apartment	£31,000	£480	£400	17%
3 bed apartment	£48,000	£600	£600	15%
3 bed townhouse	£90,000	£1100	£1100	14.6%
Detached	£100,000	£1000	£1000	12%

Demand for letting	Peak High		Off peak High	

Finance and leisure scores	Financial (out of 5) 4	Leisure (out of 5) 3	Total (out of 10) 7

Flights scheduled from	London Airports

Typical cost of flights	Peak £200–400	Off peak £130–350

Operators	British Airways, Air Malta, Alitalia

▶

Description	Gozo lies about 5 km from the north west of Malta. It enjoys warm summers and mild winters and this makes it the ideal holiday destination at any time of the year. Its motto in Latin is *Fertilis ab undis caput effero*, meaning 'a fruitful land rising its head from the sea'.
	Yields are very good. It's possible to do very well if you gear up the investment and benefit from the low borrowing rate. It makes a good alternative holiday home to the normal Spain or Cyprus off-plans and re-sales that we get rammed down our throats.
	It's not that easy to get to but you can get cheap helicopter flights and a ferry runs every other hour. For those looking for a quiet retreat, not looking to spend too much money and wanting to make an immediate healthy return then Gozo would be an obvious choice.
Hot website	www.gozo.gov.mt

Estate agents:

Name	Address	Tel	Web
Christy's Gozo Properties		(+356) 21 55 90 84	guidegozo.com/ agenzija/ ghalvin@yahoo.com
Dhalia Real Estate			http://www.dhalia. com/
Property Line Malta	37, Republic Street, Victoria, Gozo (near Maltacom)	(+356) 21 56 66 90	www.property linemalta.com info@propertyline malta.com

Letting agents:

Name	Address	Tel	Web
Dhalia Real Estate			http://www.dhalia. com/
Property Line Malta	37, Republic Street, Victoria, Gozo (near Maltacom)	(+356) 21 56 66 90	www.propertyline malta.com info@propertyline malta.com

Hungary, Budapest

Country data	
Population	10.11 million
Population growth	−0.320%
Land area	92,340 sq km
Currency and exchange rate	1 forint (Ft) = 100 filler (1 Ft ~1/380 GBP)
GDP-PPP method	US$81,183.0 millions
GDP growth	4.14%
GDP per head	US$8,033.0 thousands per person

Financial	Interest rate 8.5%	Inflation rate 5.3%

National bank	National Bank of Hungary
Political	Politics in Hungary are confrontational; Parliament is the focus of lively debate on most issues, though usually with a greater focus on political advantage than on real differences over basic policies. The presidency assumes very little executive power. In May 2004 Hungary was one of ten countries that entered into the European Union. For the foreseeable future Hungarian politics will continue to be substantially influenced by integration with the EU and the attendant economic and structural reforms. Such transformations will increasingly integrate its economy with those of its immediate neighbours as well as West European countries.
Social security	Yes
Languages	Hungarian is the major language; German, Romani, Romainian, Slovak, Slovenian, Serbian and Croatian are also spoken by various minorities.
Ethnic make-up	Hungarian 90.0%; Roma 4.0%; German 3.0%; Serb 2.0%; Romanian 1.0%

Tax	Income Tax			Capital Gains Tax
	Taxable income (HUF)	Tax on lower amount	Rate on excess	Capital Gains are taxed at a flat rate of 20%
	Exceeding (HUF) / Not exceeding (HUF)	(HUF)	%	
	0 — 600,000	0	20	
	600,000 — 1,200,000	120,000	30	
	1,200,000 — –	300,000	40	

▶

Description	After 1989 Hungary embarked on a free-market economy. The rapid privatisations caused a dip macro economically and the government implemented an austerity package to address structural problems and combat inflation. Since 1997 economic growth has been impressive with the Hungarian economy recording growth rates around 4% a year. Household and public demands have been picking up since 2001. This has been led by an export-orientated boom in manufacturing. Unemployment is quite low at around 8%. In 2002 nearly 90% of the GDP was generated from the private sector as opposed to just 10% in 1990. Major industries: metallurgy, processed food, textiles, chemicals, construction, motor vehicles, logistics and business centres. Exports have steadily risen since 1993, and over 75% of trade is now with the European Union. With EU accession trade links within the EU will further improve Hungary's economic progress.

Local data				
Investor profile	Cash & equity investor; pension investor; downshifter investor; business investor			
Category	Bronze			

Population	Total 1,775,203		British 10,000	

Climate	Hours of sunshine per day in summer	Average rainfall per year	Average temperature January	Average temperature July	Average water temperature
	9	35 days	−1.6°C	22°C	–

Proximity to	**Airport:** Budapest Ferihegy Airport is located 24km (15 miles) southeast of Budapest. **Beach:** N/A **Nearest city:** Szentendre

Restaurants and bars	New clubs and discos are constantly sprouting up all over Budapest and there is no district especially renowned for its nightlife. The bars offer something for everybody – from sleazy sex bars to calm cafés. Many bars are open until dawn, although most close at around 0400. Borozos are cheap wine cellars, where it is rare to see women, especially unaccompanied. Sorozos are beer houses that will also serve good and moderately priced food. The minimum drinking age is 18 years. Alcohol is inexpensive.

Sports and leisure facilities	The Hungarians excel at kayak and canoeing, fencing, water polo, swimming and modern pentathlon but flop in tennis, basketball and football. The most important annual event is *Hungaroring* (the Hungarian Grand Prix), which draws fans from all over Europe. Certain parts of Budapest are well set up for cycling, including both city and parks.

Transport	**Public transport:** Public transport in Budapest is excellent by international standards. You can also reach Budapest by train, including overnight direct trains from Paris and Brussels.

▶

	Roads: You should think carefully before hiring a car or driving in Budapest unless you know the city well. Traffic jams are frequent, and roads are often closed near construction sites. You can use the highway from Vienna, which was finished just a couple of years ago.
Crime rate	Since the fall of Communism, the authorities have had a difficult time controlling the growth of organised crime, but as an expat you are not likely to encounter this unless it is your lifelong dream to own a bar or a strip joint. The only crime a Western traveller is likely to experience is pickpocketing.
Main types of employment	Engineering, pharmaceutical, electronics and computer industries, manufacturing, tourism.
Future plans	Communism is well and truly history – the young are eager to adopt Western European values, while remaining in an obsessive relationship with Hungary's fascinating past. The traditions and history of the Magyar people are still vitally important, as is the ubiquitous mobile phone.
Yield range	7–10%

Type of property	Entry price	Rent – peak	Rent – off peak	Average annual yield
2 bed apartment	£35,000	£300	£300	9.1%
3 bed apartment	£50,000	£370	£370	8.8%
3 bed townhouse	£60,000	£380	£380	7.6%
Detached	£70,000	£450	£450	7.7%

Demand for letting	Peak High		Off peak Moderate

Finance and leisure scores	Financial (out of 5) 2	Leisure (out of 5) 5	Total (out of 10) 7

Flights scheduled from	London, Manchester, Birmingham, Glasgow, Newcastle and some smaller airports. Easyjet also flies from London Luton.

Typical cost of flights	Peak £140–450	Off peak £80–200

Operators	Malév, Aeroflot, Air France, British Airways, KLM and Lufthansa

Description	Buda and Pest were separate cities and the Danube was their frontier. Since 1874, the two parts – the lovely Buda hills to the west and the sprawling urban plain of Pest to the east – have been connected by municipal government. Panoramically divided by the Danube, Budapest is one of Europe's most beautiful capitals. A grand metropolis of classic coffee houses, art, sights and museums. The city was made for wandering and discovery. The joining of the EU will have an effect on property prices in the long run. It's a great place to put your money. Capital growth has to happen as the city is too thriving for it not to. Major private investment has gone in in anticipation of a rapid increase in tourists. Yields are unexciting but enough to cover the mortgage.

▶

Hot website	www.budapest.com		
Estate agents:			
Name	**Address**	**Tel**	**Web**
Casaro	1051 Budapest, Sas u. 4	+36 1 486 3500	www.casaro-hungary.com info@casaro-hungary.com
IREC			www.irec.hu/ indexa.htm realtor@irec.hu
Piramis Real Estate	Budapest, 1025 Verecke út 8	+36 1 33 55 965	www.piramis ingatlan.hu
HEURÉKA	22 Ingatlanközvetíto Bt, Budapest	+ 36 1 227 0391	www.heureka22.h heu22@axelero.hu
Letting agents:			
Name	**Address**	**Tel**	**Web**
Casaro	1051 Budapest, Sas u. 4	+36 1 486 3500	www.casaro-hungary.com info@casaro-hungary.com
Piramis Real Estate	Budapest, 1025 Verecke út 8	+36 1 33 55 965	www.piramis ingatlan.hu

Ireland, Kinsale, County Donegal

Country data	
Population	3.84 million
Population growth	1.15%
Land area	68,890 sq km
Currency and exchange rate	1 Euro = 100 cents (~0.664547 GBP)
GDP-PPP method	US$81,484.0 millions
GDP growth	4.70%
GDP per head	US$21,215.0 thousands per person

Financial	Interest rate 2%	Inflation rate 4.6%

National bank	Central Bank and Financial Services Authority of Ireland
Political	The British and Irish Governments have worked very closely together for many years on Northern Ireland issues. This led to the 1998 Belfast Agreement. Simultaneous referendums were held in Ireland and Northern Ireland in 1998. In the former people were asked to vote not only on the Belfast Agreement but also on an amendment of their constitution ending the territorial claim to Northern Ireland. Ninety-four % voted in favour of the Agreement and constitutional change. Northern Ireland Devolution took place in 1999.
Social security	Yes
Languages	Irish (Gaelic); English
Customaries	The Irish are gregarious people, and everywhere animated *craic* (talk) can be heard. Close community contact is very much part of the Irish way of life and almost everywhere there is an intimate small-town atmosphere. Pubs are often the heart of a community's social life. Visitors will find the people very friendly and welcoming no matter where one finds oneself in the country. A meal in an Irish home is usually a substantial affair and guests will eat well. Dinner is the main meal of the day and is now eaten in the evening. Handshaking is usual, and modes of address will often be informal. Smoking has been banned in all public places.
Ethnic make-up	Celtic; English

▶

Tax	Income Tax				Capital Gains Tax
	The Irish tax year changed to a calendar-year basis as of the 1st January 2002. Non-residents are taxed the same as residents.				Capital gains are taxed at a rate of 20%.
	Single or widowed individuals				
	Taxable income (€)		Tax on lower amount	Rate on excess	
	Exceeding (€)	Not exceeding (€)	(€)	%	
	0	28,000	0	20	
	28,000	–	5,600	42	
	Married couple joint assessment				
	Taxable income (€)		Tax on lower amount	Rate on excess	
	Exceeding (€)	Not exceeding (€)	(€)	%	
	0	37,000	0	20	
	37,000	–	7,400	42	
Description	The US is Ireland's largest single trading partner, along with the UK, Germany and France. Major industries: computer software, information technology, food and drink, pharmaceuticals, tourism. The Irish economy, while quite small by EU standards, nonetheless outperformed all OECD countries in real GDP growth over the last six years by a wide margin. A competitive tax regime, ready access to EU markets as well as a low cost and well-educated labour force attracted substantial new high technology investment. Historically, Ireland suffered from high unemployment, high dependency ratios and the chronic loss of talented youth to emigration. Policy changes dramatically reversed these conditions in the late 1980s and formed the foundation of the robust Irish expansion of the past 15 years. The median age in Ireland is now approximately 30 years, easily the EU's lowest. The percentage of the population classified as dependent also is well below the EU average and its GDP per capita level has crossed over the EU average. Irish foresight in investing in its educational systems in previous years is now producing major dividends. Ireland is actively recruiting skilled external labour outside the EU and has been issuing record numbers of work permits to supplement the domestic workforce. Ireland has worked a miracle in transforming its economy.				

Local data				
Investor profile	Cash & equity investor; pension investor; holiday investor; retirement investor; downshifter investor			
Category	Bronze			
Population	**Total** 35,000		**British** 250	

Climate	Hours of sunshine per day in summer	Average rainfall per year	Average temperature January	Average temperature July	Average water temperature
	5	150 days	7°C	17°C	13°C

Proximity to	**Airport:** Cork Airport 13 miles/21 kilometres **Beach:** Castlepark Marina Centre, 2 miles out of town. A lovely sandy beach two minutes' walk from the centre. **Nearest city:** Cork city 18 miles
Restaurants and bars	Kinsale is a well-known gourmet centre – it even has a gourmet festival which is generally held during the first and second weeks in October (if you plan to stay or eat here, then book well in advance) and has numerous good – and expensive – restaurants. This quaint town is small enough to make wandering the streets and browsing the menus in the windows an attractive proposition. 　　Kinsale has the complement of convivial bars that you might expect in an historic town turned tourist centre and the place is so compact that most of them are within a couple of minutes' walk of each other.
Sports and leisure facilities	Kinsale is a top class centre for sailing and watersports activity. There are three golf courses including the world-famous Old Head course. Field sports are well represented with horse riding, clay bird shooting and archery all available close to the town. 　　Castlepark Marina Centre offers deep-sea angling, scuba diving and harbour trips. At the sandy beach two minutes' walk away from the centre you can rent wind-surfing equipment, dinghies and canoes at very reasonable prices.
Transport	**Public transport:** Connections to all major rail-linked towns and cities in the country can be made from Cork's Kent Station. Eleven trains operate daily to Dublin with connections to Limerick and the West of Ireland. Several trains operate from Dublin to all major towns and cities in Northern Ireland. 　　Kinsale taxis can collect and return visitors to Cork airport, Cork railway station, Ringaskiddy Ferryport or visiting cruise ships. **Roads:** The journey from Cork to Kinsale must be made by taxi, hire car or bus. The roads are in good condition with full accessibility.
Crime rate	Low
Main types of employment	Tourism and leisure are the main employers, though there is a broad range of manufacturing and agriculture businesses.

▶

Future plans	As the 'gourmet capital of Ireland', Kinsale intends to build on and improve its tourism services in addition to sustaining an environmentally aware approach.
	In addition to this, the planned expansion of Cork Airport will add to the demand for property in Kinsale. The town has attracted a growing number of commuters who work in the UK. The quality of life and the high standard of education available is proving tempting. Some believe this trend will continue to grow.

Yield range	4–6%			
Type of property	**Entry price**	**Rent – peak**	**Rent – off peak**	**Average annual yield**
2 bed apartment	€200,000	€1000 p/m	€700 p/m	5.1%
3 bed apartment	€210,000	€1000 p/m	€700 p/m	4.85%
3 bed townhouse	€210,000	€1000 p/m	€700 p/m	4.85%
Detached	€250,000	€1200 p/m	€800 p/m	4.8%

Demand for letting	**Peak**		**Off peak**
	Very high		High

Finance and leisure scores	**Financial** (out of 5)	**Leisure** (out of 5)	**Total** (out of 10)
	2	4	6

Flights scheduled from	London and most major cities. Connection through Dublin.	

Typical cost of flights	**Peak**	**Off peak**
	£140–220	£80–150

Operators	Aer Lingus, British Airways, Lufthansa

Description	Kinsale can easily claim its place amongst Ireland's most historic locations. The estuary of the Bandon River gave it great importance as the river is tidal as far as Innishannon and water transport was dominant until the 18th century. The town nestles between the hills and the shoreline, a maze of narrow streets, never far from the water and little changed in many hundreds of years. Amongst buildings of later periods are those with historic links to the French, Spanish, British and Americans. The town has a number of excellent galleries and design shops, with an emphasis on ceramics, pottery and glass. The Good Food Circle promotes the gourmet efforts of ten or so restaurants.
	This is a safe investment. The area is already developed so voids will be minimal. The yields are low so I would not recommend that you gear up more than 50% Loan To Value as interest rises will hurt. This area will give you a solid return as there is strong demand from the influx of contract workers and will offer you above average capital growth as the prices are lower than the rest of Ireland.

Hot website	http://www.kinsale.ie/

Estate agents:			
Name	**Address**	**Tel**	**Web**
Michael Galvin Estate Agents	Market Buildings, Bandon, West Cork	+353 (23) 44958	http://www.mgalvin. ie/ email mgalvin.ie
Margaret Buckley, Kinsale Estate Agents	Pearse Street, Kinsale, Co Cork	+353 (21) 774297	kinsaleestate agents@eircom.net
O'Neills	Market Street, Kinsale, Co Cork	+353 (21) 4772168	http://www.o-neill.ie/ Info@ONeill Estates.com
Sheehy Brothers Estate Agents	Market St, Kinsale, Co Cork,	+353 (21) 4772338	www.sheehybrothers. com info@sheehybrothers. com
Letting agents:			
Name	**Address**	**Tel**	**Web**
Michael Galvin Estate Agents	Market Buildings, Bandon, West Cork,	023 44958	http://www.mgalvin. ie/ email mgalvin.ie
Sheehy Brothers Estate Agents	Market St, Kinsale, Co Cork,	+353 (21) 4772338	www.sheehybrothers. com info@sheehybrothers. com

Italy, Isola d'Elba, Tuscany

Country data		
Population	57.68 million	
Population growth	0.080 %	
Land area	294,020 sq km	
Currency and exchange rate	1 Euro = 100 cents (~0.664547 GBP)	
GDP-PPP method	US$1,188,770.0 millions	
GDP growth	1.72 %	
GDP per head	US$20,610.0 Thousands per person	
Financial	Interest rate 2%	Inflation rate 2.6%
National bank	Banca d'Italia	
Political	The centre right coalition led by Silvio Berlusconi was elected in 2001 with a strongly reformist agenda, including promises to cut taxes, stimulate new jobs and to create a more liberalised labour market. Italy held the Presidency of the EU from July to December 2003 and is playing a prominent role in the fight against international terrorism and reconstruction in Iraq, Afghanistan and the Balkans.	
Social security	Yes	
Languages	Italian (official), German, French, Slovene	
Customaries	The handshake is the standard greeting upon meeting and departure. Even children are encouraged to shake hands. In social settings, people may kiss on both cheeks. Formality is still appreciated. Use the formal form of address unless invited to move to a first name basis. Younger people move to less formal forms of address quickly. Body language is quite interesting in Italy, and because much gesticulation tends to take place, one should be aware of the commonly used gestures.	
Ethnic make-up	Italian; German; French; Slovene; Albanian; Greek	

Tax	Income Tax			Capital Gains Tax
	Non-residents are taxed on income produced within Italy at the same rates as residents.			Capital gains not realised from business activities are subject to a specific capital gains tax at a rate of 12.5%.
	Taxable income (€)		Tax on lower amount	Rate on excess	
	Exceeding (€)	Not exceeding	(€)	%	
	0	10,329	0	18	
	10,329	15,494	1,859	22	
	15,494	30,987	2,995	32	
	30,987	69,722	7,953	38	
	69,722	–	22,672	44	

Description	Italy is the fourth largest economy in Western Europe and the world's seventh largest. Policies introduced in the early 1990s helped prepare the country for a smooth transition to the Eurozone, and its decision to join the Euro has improved investor confidence significantly. Major industries: tourism, machinery, clothing, engineering, chemicals, textiles and motor vehicles. Major trading partners: the EU (in particular Germany, France and the UK) and the US. The south of the country, the Mezziogiorni, has a much lower economic output and suffers higher unemployment rates than the more industrialised north. The country's standard of living is high, particularly in the north, where unemployment is extremely low and per capita income is amongst Europe's highest.

Local data

Investor profile	Cash & equity investor; pension investor; holiday investor; retirement investor; downshifter investor; business investor
Category	Bronze

Population	Total 30,000	British 200

Climate:	Hours of sunshine per day in summer	Average rainfall per year	Average temperature January	Average temperature July	Average water temperature
	9	55 days	17°C	27°C	23°C

Proximity to	**Airport:** Pisa Airport – and then either connection to Aeroporto La Pila in Marina di Campo, or drive direct from Pisa Airport to Piombino Marittima. The only way to go to Elba from here is to take the boat. Elba does have an airport nearby, but only caters for a few flights from privileged European cities. **Beach:** Fetovaia beach, Seccheto beach, Cavoli beach **Nearest city:** Fetovaia

Restaurants and bars	The island has some good restaurants, including Mexican. Tourists often try some of Elba's best wines in wine cellars which are located just by the seaside.
Sports and leisure facilities	Swimming, riding, golf and trekking, hiking, botanical walks, bird watching and tennis. The island is also a nice place to go for fishing activities or sailing.
Transport	**Public transport:** You can reach the island of Elba by car to Piombino, then take a ferry across to the Island. The island offers regular bus services around the beaches in addition to water taxis and minibuses to the beaches. **Roads:** The roads are in good shape and are used by buses, taxis and cars.
Crime rate	Very low
Main types of employment	Tourism and services
Future plans	To improve upon its thriving tourism industry and preserve the rich natural history of the island
Yield range	6–9%

Type of property	**Entry price**	**Rent – peak**	**Rent – off peak**	**Average annual yield**
2 bed apartment	£45,000	£400	£250	8.6%
3 bed apartment	£60,000	£500	£300	8%
3 bed townhouse	£65,000	£500	£300	7.3%
Detached	£75,000	£550	£300	6.4%

Demand for letting	**Peak** High		**Off peak** Moderately high	

Finance and leisure scores	**Financial** (out of 5) 3	**Leisure** (out of 5) 3	**Total** (out of 10) 6

Flights scheduled from	London, Manchester, Birmingham, Liverpool, Coventry, Newcastle, Luton and some other regional airports

Typical cost of flights	**Peak** £70–120	**Off peak** £40–90

Operators	Alitalia, British Airways, Ryanair, Britannia, Mytravellite and other low cost airlines
Description	Elba is rich in memories of her tormented past: archaeological finds, military structures, Napoleon's residences, and then, under the sea along the coastline, the remains of ships that transported Elba's wine to Mediterranean centres. Elba is a rich source of history, archaeology and treasures. It's very cheap to get here as there are many low cost airlines flying to this area. Yields are okay and entry prices are reasonable compared to other countries such as Spain or Portugal. Capital Gains Tax is set at a low rate thus exiting from the investment will not hit the bottom line too hard.

▶

Hot website	www.elba-online.com		
Estate agents			
Name	**Address**	**Tel**	**Web**
Tuscany Invest	Via L.da Vinci, 15 57029, Venturina (Li), Tuscany	0039 0565 3872	www.tuscany invest.com info@tuscany invest.com
Elba Island I Ginepri	Rione de Gasperi, 24 57031 Capoliveri (Li), Tuscany	0039 0565 96 87 75	http://www.elba island.com/
Agenzia Immobiliare Meditur	Viale Cerboni, 2 Marciana Marina (LI) Tuscany	0039 0565 904136	www.immobiliare-meditur.it info@immobiliare-meditur.it
Immobiliare Elba	Via Mellini, 26 57031, Capoliveri, Tuscany	0039 0565 935141	www.immobiliare-elba.com info@immobiliare-elba.com
Letting agents			
Name	**Address**	**Tel**	**Web**
Elba Island I Ginepri	Rione de Gasperi, 24 57031 Capoliveri (Li), Tuscany	0039 0565 96 87 75	http://www.elba island.com/
Agenzia Immobiliare Meditur	Viale Cerboni 2, Marciana Marina, (LI) Tuscany	0039 0565 904136	www.immobiliare-meditur.it info@immobiliare-meditur.it

Poland, Krakow

Country data			
Population	38.63 million		
Population growth	−0.030%		
Land area	304,510 sq km		
Currency and exchange rate	1 zlotych (Zl$) = 100 groszy (~0.143 GBP)		
GDP-PPP method	US$271,945.0 millions		
GDP growth	1.03%		
GDP per head	US$7,039.0 thousands per person		
Financial	Interest rate 2%		Inflation rate 3.2%
National bank	National Bank of Poland		
Political	Under the new constitution that came into force in October 1997, the legislative power in Poland is vested in a bicameral national assembly consisting of a 460-seat lower assembly and 100-seat upper assembly. Elections are by proportional representation.		
Social security	Yes		
Languages	Polish		
Customaries	The Polish are friendly, hard-working people and are very pleasant when meeting foreigners. However, one should take note that there are vast differences between traditions and practices between people in the cities such as Krakow and the little rural villages. Catholicism plays an integral part in everyday life. Shaking hands upon meeting a person is the norm. Smoking is restricted in some public buildings. You should also note that taking photographs of military installations could land you in trouble.		
Ethnic make-up	Polish 97.0%; German 1.0%; Ukrainian 1.0%; Byelorussian 1.0%		

Tax	Income Tax			Capital Gains Tax
	Non-residents are subject to a final withholding tax of 20% on fees received for membership on management boards, commission, service and management contracts, interest, copyrights, trademarks, designs and know-how.			Taxed at a flat rate of 10%

Taxable income (PLN)		Tax on lower amount	Rate on excess
Exceeding (PLN)	Not exceeding (PLN)	(PLN)	%
0	37,024	0	19
37,024	74,048	6,516.	30
74,048	–	17,623	40

▶

Description	A return to the socialist led government does not seem to have the potential to disturb the future of a vibrant Polish economy. However, market reforms and general reform attempts have caused some social disruption and persistently high unemployment rates, currently at around 18% and rising.
	On a historical note, Poland was the first country in the central bloc to regain the levels of GDP that it had enjoyed before the fall of communism.
	Major industries: machine building, iron and steel, coal, shipbuilding, glass, beverages, chemicals, textiles and food processing. Major trading partners: Germany, Italy, the Netherlands, Russia, Ukraine, France and the UK.
	Public finance reform is important for Poland's long-term economic outlook. A new initiative proposed sets to rationalise public finances and cut social spending.

Local data				

Investor profile	Cash & equity investor; pension investor; holiday investor; retirement investor; downshifter investor; business investor; university investor			
Category	Bronze			

Population	Total		British	
	734,400 (2002)		8,000	

Climate	Hours of sunshine per day in summer	Average rainfall per year	Average temperature January	Average temperature July	Average water temperature
	7	450mm	0°C/33°F	21°C/71°F	N/a

Proximity to	**Airport:** Krakow's *John Paul II International Airport* of Balice is situated conveniently on the outskirts of the city, just 15 km (about 10 miles) from its centre.
	Beach: N/a
	Nearest city: Katowice

Restaurants and bars	There is no shortage of places to drink, eat, and stay merry late into the night in Krakow. The huge central Grand Square in the heart of the historic Old Town district, and its environs, look like they never sleep most of the year save winter. Trendy new hangouts are launched in the nearby Kazimierz quarter almost by the month.
	Krakow has always been Poland's gourmet Mecca. Last decade brought a restaurant explosion all over the city.

Sports and leisure facilities	Sadly, sport is not the routine of an average Krakow dweller. The city abounds in fine jogging paths but few natives take advantage of it. Also bikeways crisscrossing metropolitan Krakow and its environs seem underused despite the city's vocal group of ardent cyclists. Hiking remains the most popular outdoor activity, and no wonder seeing that the Krakow region is famous for its beauty.
	Hunting and fishing are centuries-sanctioned sports in Poland. Both – especially the latter – retain considerable following in Krakow.

▶

Transport	**Public transport:** Krakow is one of Poland's main railroad junctions with five trunk lines. Its central Krakow Glowny station is in the very city centre, close to the Old Town historic district. Expresses run to all major cities in Poland. Most convenient is the shuttle express service to and from capital Warsaw. In addition expresses arrive from Berlin, Dresden, Frankfurt, Leipzig, Vienna, Prague, Budapest, Bucharest, Bratislava, Kosice, Kiev, Lvov and Odessa.
	Roads: With the city's abundant road connections, no other major city in Poland can boast better accessibility from abroad. Krakow lies at one of the key European crossroads, en route from the West via Germany to the East via Ukraine and from Scandinavia to the Mediterranean via Austria. Within Poland bus companies compete fiercely on the most popular routes. And in the Krakow region minibus services have become the chief means of commuting apart from car.
Crime rate	Poland is generally safer than most European countries, east or west. And Krakow is safer than other major cities in Poland. Petty crime seems pretty common in the city and whereas mugging remains sporadic, pilfering is rampant.
Main types of employment	Krakow is Poland's fourth biggest manufacturing centre, with steel, tobacco and pharmaceuticals being the key industries. The city is second only to the capital Warsaw as regards the service sector.
Future plans	Poland's labour costs stay at a third of Germany's, and the country boasts a sizeable and fast-expanding internal market, enjoys a healthy GDP growth, and remains a model of political and economic stability in the region. With many foreign investors already (and investors flocking from across Europe after EU accession), from multinationals to fairly small enterprises, Krakow appears a particularly good place with some 8.5 million people living within a radius of 100 km. The city is situated at Europe's crucial crossroads between Germany and Ukraine and between Scandinavia and the south of the continent.
Yield range	6–8%

Type of property	Entry price	Rent – peak	Rent – off peak	Average annual yield
2 bed apartment	£22,000	£150	£140	8%
3 bed apartment	£34,000	£240	£190	7.7%
3 bed townhouse	£33,000	£240	£190	8%
Detached	£50,000	£290	£250	6.5%

Demand for letting	Peak High		Off peak Medium	

Finance and leisure scores	Financial (out of 5) 2	Leisure (out of 5) 4	Total (out of 10) 6

Flights scheduled from	Most major cities throughout the UK. Some smaller airlines from regional airports.

Typical cost of flights	Peak £100–£230	Off peak £80–£170

Operators	Austrian Airlines, British Airways, British Midland Airways, Lufthansa, and Malev fly passengers to Krakow besides the Polish national carrier LOT.
Description	Krakow is Poland's capital of culture. The city boasts the best museums in the country and some of the best theatres. It counts two Nobel Prize winners in literature among its residents. It is also home to one of the world's oldest and most distinguished universities. No wonder Krakow was named a European City of Culture in 2000. Entry prices are low and there's lots to do here. There's a vibrancy to this area and you'll have no problem letting your place to those young city professionals. The list of airlines flying to this area is growing month by month and flight prices are falling. I reckon Easyjet and Rynair will be flying here soon. This will increase demand for these properties I'm sure. Above average capital gain is likely.
Hot website	www.krakow-info.com

Estate agents:

Name	Address	Tel	Web
Firma Kontrakty Nieruchomości	Plac Wolnica 9, 31-060 Krakow	(+48 12) 2920016	www.fk-nieruchomosci.pl biuro@fk-nieruchomosci.pl
Katarzyna Turek, Inwestycje Finanse Nieruchomości	Morawskiego 10/1A, 30-102 Krakow	+48509108248	schmidt@ifn.pl www.ifn.pl.
Ober-Haus Real Estate Agency	ul.Slawkowska 6, 31-014 Krakow ul.Wadowicka 6, 30-415 Krakow	(+4812) 4281700 (+4812) 2679100	www.ober-haus.pl
Anna Kubacka Nieruchomości	ul.Krakowska 7/11, 31-062 Kraków	(+4812) 2920265	magnat@informer.pl

Letting agents:

Name	Address	Tel	Web
Firma Kontrakty Nieruchomości	Plac Wolnica 9, 31-060 Krakow	(+48 12) 2920016	www.fk-nieruchomosci.pl biuro@fk-nieruchomosci.pl
Katarzyna Turek, Inwestycje Finanse Nieruchomości	Morawskiego 10/1A, 30 102 Krakow	+48509108248	schmidt@ifn.pl www.ifn.pl.

Portugal, Lagos, Redondo		
Country data		
Population	10.07 million	
Population growth	0.180%	
Land area	91,640 sq km	
Currency and exchange rate	1 Euro = 100 cents (~0.664 GBP)	
GDP-PPP method	US$148,785.0 millions	
GDP growth	1.52%	
GDP per head	US$14,781.0 thousands per person	
Financial	Interest rate 2%	Inflation rate 3.3%
National bank	Banco de Portugal	
Political	The government has been a republic since 1910. The coalition government's programme includes cutting public expenditure and making public accounts more transparent, while meeting the terms and conditions of the European growth and stability pact. The government has pushed ahead with an economic programme of reform designed to reduce the budget deficit, despite public opposition and economic recession.	
Social security	Yes	
Languages	Portuguese, English spoken in business areas	
Customaries	Often overshadowed by its much larger eastern neighbour, Spain, Portugal has its own distinct language, identity, customs, landscapes and scenery. Despite the encroachment of tourism, it remains one of the least spoilt corners of Europe. The Portuguese way of life is leisurely, and old-fashioned politeness is essential. Warm, Latin hospitality is the norm. The country has a deeply individual national character, although each province has its own traditions and folklore. Casual wear is widely acceptable, although beachwear should not be worn in towns. In restaurants, it is usual to smoke only at the end of the meal. Smoking is prohibited in cinemas, theatres and on buses.	
Ethnic make-up	99% Portuguese, 1% African	

Tax	Income Tax			Capital Gains Tax
	Non-residents are subject to personal income tax arising on income in Portugal. Individuals are considered resident if they have a dwelling in Portugal, which may imply their intention to use it as their habitual residence.			Taxable capital gains that are not specifically exempt or taxed separately are taxed at the ordinary rates listed. Capital gains derived from a personal residence are tax exempt if the proceeds are reinvested in another personal residence in Portugal within 24 months after the sale or 12 months prior to the sale.
	Taxable income (€)		Tax on lower amount	Rate on excess
	Exceeding (€)	Not exceeding (€)	(€)	%
	0	4,100	0	12
	4,100	6,201	492	14
	6,201	15,375	786	24
	15,375	35,363	2,987	34
	35,363	51,251	9,783	38
	51,251	–	15,821	40

Description	Portugal has traditionally based its economy on textiles, wine, clothing, wood products, metalworking and chemicals. However, a recent boom in the electronics, energy and telecommunications sectors has helped the economy. These are likely to continue expanding and helping to broaden the economic base.
	Major trading partners: the US, Brazil and the EU. With its integration into the EU economy, Portugal achieved a dramatic economic turnaround from the early 1970s. During the last ten years, the Portuguese economy has achieved some of the highest growth rates amongst EU and OECD countries. Portugal is the UK's 26th largest export market with the UK being one of the biggest foreign investors in Portugal.

Local data	
Investor profile	Cash & equity investor; pension investor; holiday investor; retirement investor; downshifter investor; business investor
Category	Gold

Population	Total 90,000		British 2300	

Climate	Hours of sunshine per day in summer	Average rainfall per year	Average temperature January	Average temperature July	Average water temperature
	12	17 days	15°C/59F	28°C/82F	20°C

Proximity to	**Airport:** 100 km Arrive at Lisbon or Faro and make your journey towards Lagos by bus. **Beach:** Meia Praia, Praia d'Ana and Porto do Mos **Nearest city:** Portimao

▶

Restaurants and bars	Searching out new restaurants is marvellous, most have tables outdoors in season, set beneath fragrant orange trees in the square or lined along the edges of the narrow streets. There is a fantastic selection with many specialising in fresh fish, which is delicious. Lagos has an excellent nightlife, centred around the old town. Wandering through the maze of winding streets soaking up the atmosphere is entertainment enough but you will come across a good choice of bars and discos.
Sports and leisure facilities	Windsurfing at Meia Praia, and the Praia da Luz Sea Sports Centre offers scuba-diving, sailing, fishing and snorkelling. Tennis, squash, swimming pools and a bowling green. The Palmares 18-hole golf course is situated east of Lagos. Bird-watching can be arranged at various protected reserves in the area.
Transport	**Public transport:** Good network of buses and taxis available **Roads:** New roads that have made travel faster
Crime rate	Very low
Main types of employment	Services and tourism. Some farming.
Future plans	In some areas, property prices have risen by nearly 40% in the past two years. Still billed as one of the cheapest areas in Western Europe, the prices are slowly starting to rise.
Yield range	12–21%

Type of property	Entry price	Rent – peak	Rent – off peak	Average annual yield
2 bed apartment	£40,000	£800	£600	21%
3 bed apartment	£70,000	£900	£800	13%
3 bed townhouse	£130,000	£1100	£1100	10%
Detached	£100,000	£1100	£900	12%

Demand for letting	Peak Very high		Off peak Moderately high	

Finance and leisure scores	Financial (out of 5) 5	Leisure (out of 5) 4	Total (out of 10) 9

Flights scheduled from	All major cities and some smaller airlines fly to the Algarve from smaller cities. Many flights frequent this part of Portugal from the UK as it is a popular holiday destination for Brits.

Typical cost of flights	Peak £100–200	Off peak £60–100

Operators	Easyjet, Ryanair, Basiqair, Air Luxor, First Choice holidays, Air2000
Description	Lagos is the third largest town in the Algarve, straddling the river Bensafrim and surrounded by the most beautiful, unspoilt countryside. It's a spacious town with a maze of winding cobbled streets full of pavement restaurants, café bars, antique and art shops.

▶

	Yields are very high for the smaller sized properties so go for these. Inflation is a little bit high which should help property prices along and increase above the national rate. I struggle to find what's wrong with this place. If I was pushed I would say that demand tails off for some of the off peak season. Otherwise the yields are great, the properties are of good value, there's loads to do, it has low crime rates and it's easy to get to – what more do you want!
Hot website	http://www.valegrifo.com/vglagos.htm

Estate agents:

Name	Address	Tel	Web
RS Propriedades	Rua Dr. Paulo J. Godinho, Lote 5 – Loja C, 8600-774, Lagos	+351 282-768-821	www.portugal-forsale.com
Portugal Villa			www.portugalvilla.com manors@manorhouses.com
NonPlusUltra	Sociedade de Mediação Imobilaria, Lda. Parque de Moinho, Lote 1 B, Loja D, 8600-719 Lagos	+351 282 764 771	www.nonplusultra-lda.com/en/ info@nonplusultra-lda.com

Letting agents:

Name	Address	Tel	Web
Portugal Villa			www.portugalvilla.com manors@manorhouses.com
NonPlusUltra	Sociedade de Mediação Imobilaria, Lda. Parque de Moinho, Lote 1 B, Loja D, 8600-719 Lagos	+351 282 764 771	www.nonplusultra-lda.com/en/ info@nonplusultra-lda.com

Spain, Murcia		
Country data		
Population	40.04 million	
Population growth	0.100%	
Land area	499,400 sq km	
Currency and exchange rate	1 Euro = 100 cents (~0.664 GBP)	
GDP-PPP method	US$678,859.0 millions	
GDP growth	2.59%	
GDP per head	US$16,955.0 thousands per person	
Financial	Interest rate 2%	Inflation rate 3.6%
National bank	Banco de España	
Political	There are 17 *comunidades autonomas* (autonomous regions). These have a regional parliament and a government with varying degrees of powers on local affairs. Three regions with a tradition of autonomy and their own language – the Basque country (Euskadi), Cataluñya and Galicia – have wider powers. The Basque government, for example, raises its own taxes.	
	King Carlos became head of State upon the death of General Franco in 1975.	
	The latest elections proved to have a global interest. José Maria Aznar's Popular Party were comfortably ahead in the polls in advance of the 2004 elections. However, devastating bombs in the capital Madrid put the entire country in turmoil a few days before the elections and the Spanish Socialist Workers Party (PSOE) surprisingly won, forming a minority government.	
Social security	Yes	
Languages	Castilian Spanish, Catalan, Galician, Euskera (Basque), Valencian, Majorcan	
Customaries	Spanish life has undergone rapid change in recent years and many of the stricter religious customs are giving way to more modern ways, particularly in the cities and among women.	
	Despite this, many old customs, manners and traditions have not faded and hospitality, chivalry and courtesy remain important. Handshaking is the customary form of greeting. Normal social courtesies should be observed when visiting someone's home. Smoking is widely accepted	
Ethnic make-up	In addition to Spaniards, there are several minority groups, including Gypsies, Portuguese, Latin Americans and North Africans.	

▶

Tax	Income Tax	Capital Gains Tax
	Total tax liability consists of the tax liability computed under the general rate plus the tax liability computed under the autonomous community rates. The maximum marginal rate is 48%. Income derived from non-residents is generally subject to a final withholding tax of 25%. Capital gains from a permanent establishment are subject to a 35% final withholding tax.	Capital gains are calculated as the difference between the transfer price of an asset and its acquisition price. Acquisition prices of real estate are indexed by applying co-efficients determined by the government. Capital gains held longer than one year are taxed at a rate of 18%. For less than one year, it is taxed in the taxable income bracket.
Description	Even though Aznar has done well for Spain economically, it is still suffering from the transitional period that was necessary for EU membership. Spain still has the highest unemployment rate amongst industrialised nations in western Europe in 2003 at around 11.4%. The global slowdown has also dented the GDP of Spain and consumer confidence has dipped. Spain has a mixed economy with large agricultural and industrial sectors, and important tourism and banking industries, the vast tourism industry mainly servicing visitors from northern Europe. In addition it has fishing, construction, wine, cement, chemicals, engineering and telecommunications. Major trading partners: the EU, Latin America and Japan.	
	Local data	
Investor profile	Cash & equity investor; pension investor; holiday Investor; retirement investor; downshifter investor; business investor	
Category	Bronze	

Population	Total 1,190,000		British 2000

Climate	Hours of sunshine per day in summer	Average rainfall per year	Average temperature January	Average temperature July	Average water temperature
	10	14 days	15°C	30°C	20°C

Proximity to	**Airport:** San Javier Airport is 47 km from the city of Murcia by dual carriageway. **Beach:** Costa Calida **Nearest city:** Cartagena
Restaurants and bars	There are a great number of bars and squares where you can enjoy a delicious appetiser in the open air. Some of the most popular bars are situated in Plaza San Juan. At the weekends, the bars serving tapas in Plaza del las Flores and la Plaza Mayor are much frequented. Many bars line the pavements, with the students and academics of the town frequenting the coffee shops and bars.

▶

Sports and leisure facilities	Potholing routes through caves, horse-riding, rural activities, white-water canoeing, cave-diving, deep-sea diving, paragliding, hang-gliding.			
Transport	**Public transport:** The railway network, with the imminent incorporation of the high-speed train (AVE) connecting Murcia with Madrid and the Valencia region provides excellent facilities to reach other parts of Spain. The good bus network in Murcia itself is a viable and efficient way of travelling throughout the Murcia region. **Roads:** A lot of investment has gone into upgrading the road network, and the improvements in the construction of motorways have made it possible to enhance links between the different townships within the region and at the same time with the rest of Spain.			
Crime rate	Low			
Main types of employment	Educational, service and business			
Future plans	Licences are being finalised for a new airport near Corvera that will operate 24/7 serving an increased number of flights from England using low-cost carriers.			
Yield range	6–9%			
Type of property	Entry price	Rent – peak	Rent – off peak	Average annual yield
2 bed apartment	£40,000	£300	£230	8.1%
3 bed apartment	£45,000	£330	£230	6.9%
3 bed townhouse	£50,000	£400	£300	8.4%
Detached	£60,000	£400	£300	7%

Demand for letting	Peak Very high		Off peak High	

Finance and leisure scores	Financial (out of 5) 3	Leisure (out of 5) 4	Total (out of 10) 7

Flights scheduled from	London Stanstead, Birmingham, East Midlands, Dublin

Typical cost of flights	Peak £180–250	Off peak £50–100

Operators	Buzz, BMIbaby, Ryanair
Description	A very historic city which offers insights into everyday Spanish life, as well as a rich legacy of art and contrasting cultures. Greeks, Romans, Carthaginians, Phoenicians and Moors have all left their mark. An unexplored region yet to be fully discovered by holidaymakers. We had to include Spain! There is a constant shortage of rental properties in Murcia, especially town houses and villas for long-term lets. This has driven the price up of town house and villas due to the business investors moving in. But there are still some to be had and you'll have no problem letting them. Murcia is one of the hottest resorts and the season is almost all year round. Rental demand is consistent throughout the year and will be in

	the future. Yields will be stable for at least the next five years. There is no sign of major capital growth, even though above average within this time, but over the long term it will move above average.
Hot website	www.murcia-turismo.com

Estate agents:			
Name	**Address**	**Tel**	**Web**
Orma Inmobiliaria	Cille Juan Ramon Jimenez, Cehegin, Murcia, 30410	+34 659222091	contacto@spanish-houses-orma.com
Properties Murcia	C/Emeterio Cuadrado, 1 Bajo, 30562 Mula (Murcia),	+34 968 66 26 59	www.properties murcia.com info@properties murcia.com
Inmocentro	Gran Vía de La Manga, Urb. La Gola, local nº 1 Murcia	+34 968 56 46 76	
Improsureste, s.l.	Plaza Bohemia, 54A, Bajo A, Murcia	+34 968280310	

Letting agents:			
Name	**Address**	**Tel**	**Web**
Properties Murcia	C/Emeterio Cuadrado, 1 Bajo, 30562 Mula (Murcia)	+34 968 66 26 59	www.properties murcia.com info@properties murcia.com
Inmocentro	Gran Vía de La Manga, Urb. La Gola, local nº 1, Murcia	+34 968 56 46 76	

Turkey, Fethiye

Country data	
Population	66.49 million
Population growth	1.26%
Land area	770,760 sq km
Currency and exchange rate	Turkish lira (TL$) (~0.000000364757 GBP)
GDP-PPP method	US$381,237.0 millions
GDP growth	−8.550%
GDP per head	US$5,733.0 Thousands per person

Financial	Interest rate 5%	Inflation rate 18.4%
National bank	Türkiye Cumhuriyet Merkez Bankası	
Political	Under the constitution of 1987, legislative power is vested in a single chamber, the 550-member National Assembly, elected by proportional representation. It elects both a prime minister (normally head of the largest party in the assembly) and a president, who is head of state. Since war erupted in Iraq in 2003 four key issues have dominated the political agenda: Iraq, EU accession, Cyprus and the economy. The government have also had to deal with terrorist activity in Istanbul, ensuing in a major crackdown on such activity.	
Social security	Yes	
Languages	Turkish, Kurdish, Arabic, Albanian, Armenian, Bulgarian, Greek, Domani, Romani, Ladino, Serbian and Tartar.	
Customaries	Shaking hands is the normal form of greeting. Hospitality is very important and visitors should respect Islamic customs. Informal wear is acceptable, but beachwear should be confined to the beach or poolside. Smoking is widely acceptable but prohibited in cinemas, theatres, city buses and *dolmuses* (collective taxis).	
Ethnic make-up	Turkish 80.0%; Kurdish 20.0%	

Tax	Income Tax			Capital Gains Tax
	Taxable income (TL)		Tax rate	Generally taxed as part of normal income.
	Exceeding (TL)	Not exceeding (TL)	%	
	0	3,800	15	
	3,800	9,500	20	
	9,500	19,000	25	
	19,000	47,500	30	
	47,500	95,000	35	
	95,000	–	40	

▶

Description	Turkey benefits from both a capable workforce and diverse natural resources while occupying a strategic position linking Asia, Europe and the Middle East. Turkey's large, youthful labour pool, faced with limited domestic opportunities, has sent some two million expatriate workers into Western Europe alone. Annual remittances to Turkey from these provides about 2.5 % of GDP in 2000.
	The agricultural sector still accounts for 15% of economic output and is still a vital employment source. Tourism dominates the service sector, although it has experienced some downturn since the terrorist activity in Istanbul in 2003.
	Turkey is one of the world's most rapidly industrialising markets. The economic and political activity over the next few years will be decisive in whether Turkey can join the EU in 2007.

Local data	
Investor profile:	Cash & equity investor; pension investor; holiday investor; retirement investor; downshifter investor; business investor
Category	Silver

Population	Total 3,000	British 100

Climate	Hours of sunshine per day in summer	Average rainfall per year	Average temperature January	Average temperature July	Average water temperature
	10	20 days	12°C	34°C	20°C

Proximity to	**Airport:** Dalaman Airport – 50 km
	Beach: Calis Beach
	Nearest city: Olu Deniz

Restaurants and bars	Sitting on the café-lined harbour front, drinking Turkish tea or the local lager, you can decide which boat trip you will take tomorrow, or spend time perusing the *paspastur* – the alley ways of shops. This area is best experienced at night, when the lights, sounds and atmosphere really bring the town alive.
	There's a good balance of evening activities mainly centred around the bars along the seafront and the picturesque old quarter is packed with bazaar-style shops, restaurants and bars.

Sports and leisure facilities	In Fethiye you will find watersport activities for the more adventure seeking – rafting, sailing and paragliding over the surrounding mountains, and mountain biking.
	Fethiye has full marina and mooring facilities. Besides Fethiye, Gocek and Marmaris are the other two ports which are near to Oludeniz. Both these ports have excellent marina and yachting facilities.

Transport	**Public transport:** Fethiye is well served with most of the major bus companies within Turkey. Pamukkale, Kamil Koc, Ulusoy, Metro are some of the major bus companies which have direct services from Istanbul, Izmir Ankara, Antalya and from most other big cities.

▶

	Roads: Excellent links on good roads. The terrain can get a bit hilly and offers spectacular scenery whilst driving.
Crime rate	Low
Main types of employment	Services and tourism
Future plans	To continue building on its tourist offerings and to preserve historic roots.
Yield range	8–10%

Type of property	Entry price	Rent – peak	Rent – off peak	Average annual yield
2 bed apartment	£28,000	£270	£200	9.8%
3 bed apartment	£30,000	£280	£220	9.3%
3 bed townhouse	£28,000	£240	£190	9%
Detached	£34,000	£280	£190	8.4%

Demand for letting	Peak	Off peak
	Very high	Quite high to moderate

Finance and leisure scores	Financial (out of 5)	Leisure (out of 5)	Total (out of 10)
	4	4	8

Flights scheduled from	London Airports, Manchester, Luton, Birmingham, Newcastle, Cardiff, Belfast

Typical cost of flights	Peak	Off peak
	£170–350	£140–190

Operators	Turkish Airlines, British Airways, Thomson, Air 2000, Excel Airways
Description	Fethiye is an ancient Lycian town with relics dating back to the 4th century BC and is reputed to have been visited by Alexander the Great. Set against the magnificent backdrop of the Taurus Mountains and surrounded by a beautiful, island-strewn bay, Fethiye is a lively port and market town where Turkish life and tourism exist side by side.
	The high inflation rate can only work in your favour as yields will increase as wages do, thus increasing rental values. Yields are at a good starting point so increases on these will be most welcome. Tenant demand is strong and the likelihood of resale is high as there is a ready market for properties in this area.
Hot website	www.caroletayfun.com/turkey/fethiye/

Estate agents			
Name	Address	Tel	Web
Property-Turkey			info@property-turkey.co.uk www.property-turkey.co.uk
Apple Real Estate	Ölüdeniz/Fethiye 48300	+90 252 617 07 77	www.appleestate.co.uk info@appleestate.co.uk
Taurean properties	Baris Manco Bulvari, Calis Beach, Fethiye	+ 90 252 613 2377	www.taurean properties.co.uk
Soestates Estate Agents	Ataturk, Cad.no:20, Fethiye,	+ 90 252 6 144 452	http://www.soestates.com/
Letting agents:			
Name	Address	Tel	Web
Soestates Estate Agents	Ataturk, Cad.no:20, Fethiye	+ 90 252 6 144 452	http://www.soestates.com/
Apple Real Estate	Ölüdeniz/Fethiye, 48300	+90 252 617 07 77	www.appleestate.co.uk info@appleestate.co.uk

North America
(including Central America)

Antigua, Jolly Harbour
Barbados, St James, Turtle Beach
Mexico, Cancun
Panama, Panama City, Costa Blanca
USA, Orlando, Florida

Antigua, Jolly Harbour

Country data

Population	0.067 million
Population growth	0.760%
Land area	440 sq km
Currency and exchange rate	EC$1 = 100 cents (~0.205 GBP)
GDP-PPP method	US$500.0 millions
GDP growth	−1.350%
GDP per head	US$7,464.0 thousands per person

Financial	Interest rate 7%	Inflation rate 1%

National bank	Offshore Financial centre
Political	Antigua and Barbuda has Her Majesty Queen Elizabeth as the head of State with a Westminster style Parliament. Antigua and Barbuda became an independent member of the Commonwealth in November 1981. Government is democratically elected at least once every five years and The United Progressive Party (UPP) won elections in 2004. Relationships between the two islands are not always harmonious.
Social security	No
Languages	English (official); also Patois and various other local dialects
Customaries	It is not a good idea to wear scanty clothing or beachwear in towns or villages as it is generally not accepted.
Ethnic make-up	African ancestry; European ancestry (predominantly British and Portuguese); Arab ancestry (predominantly Syrian and Lebanese).

Tax	Income Tax No up to date published data	Capital Gains Tax No up to date published data

Description	One of the major and consistently encouraged industries is tourism, and Antigua was one the earliest of the Caribbean islands to actively promote it. Financial sector and tourism are the most important sources of economic prosperity, accounting for roughly 75% combined. However, Antigua has had some years of slightly fluctuating economic performance, primarily due to large debt. In addition, destructive hurricane patterns and concerns of post September 11 attacks had some impact on the tourism business, but is now steadily recovering. Other major industries include construction, light manufacturing, agricultural products such as cotton, fruits, bananas, coconuts and mangoes. Major trading partners are OECS, Barbados, Guyana, Trinidad and Tobago, UK, Canada and the USA.

▶

Local data				
Investor profile	Cash & equity investor; pension investor; holiday investor; retirement investor; downshifter investor; business investor			
Category	Gold			
Population	**Total** 10,000		**British** 500	
Climate	Hours of sunshine per day in summer	Average rainfall per year	Average temperature January	Average temperature July	Average water temperature
	11	42 inches	24°C (76°F)	30°C (86°F)	26°C
Proximity to	**Airport:** V.C. Bird International Airport 8km (5 miles) northeast of the capital, St John's. Jolly Harbour is a 20 minute drive from St Johns. **Beach:** As Jolly Harbour is located on a peninsula, there are two gorgeous white sand beaches. **Nearest city:** St Johns			
Restaurants and bars	There is an excellent choice locally.			
Sports and leisure facilities	Water sports include diving, sailing, exploring. Sailing is a big sport in Antigua, which is a major yachting centre that hosts the annual internationally recognized Antigua Sailing Week. Tennis and golf are also important to a select few and there is an 18-hole golf course.			
Transport	**Public transport:** There are some local bus services and taxis are available throughout Antigua. **Roads:** The roads are in good condition and offers links to most villages.			
Crime rate	Antigua is relatively crime free, but normal precautions should be exercised.			
Main types of employment	Tourism and services			
Future plans	To maintain the activities and increase tourist facilities.			
Yield range	10–15%			
Type of property	Entry price	Rent – peak	Rent – off peak	Average annual yield
2 bed apartment	£125,000	£1900	£1400	15.3%
3 bed apartment	£275,000	£3000	£2200	10.9%
3 bed townhouse	£320,000	£3000	£2900	11.6%
Detached	£350,000	£3200	£3200	10.9%
Demand for letting	**Peak** Extremely high		**Off peak** Very high	
Finance and leisure scores	**Financial** (out of 5) 4	**Leisure** (out of 5) 4	**Total** (out of 10) 8	

▶

Flights scheduled from	London Gatwick, London Heathrow, Manchester, Birmingham	
Typical cost of flights	**Peak** £800–2200	**Off Peak** £480–1200
Operators	British Airways, BWIA, Virgin Atlantic, Air 2000	
Description	Antigua is known as 'the beach with an island in the middle'. Its famed countless, silky beaches are surrounded by clear blue seas and are cooled by light breezes. Jolly Harbour offers comfortable and stylish waterfront and golf course homes and building plots, in a tropical setting of coconut palms and perennial flowers. It is expensive to get here and to buy. This is the only reason why this area did not get top marks for the financials. However, because it offers double digit yields for all property types I recommend this area for the wealthier readers: entry to the market is high. Re-sale for a property here will not be a problem and I suspect capital growth will be above average due to such healthy yields being achievable all the year round. With a low inflation rate, a sensible interest rate and relative political stability I would shoot this area to the top of your list if you are considering the Caribbean cities only.	
Hot website	www.antigua-barbuda.com/tourists	

Estate agents:

Name	Address	Tel	Web
Jolly Harbour Villa Sales	PO Box 1793, St John's, Antigua, West Indies	+268 462 3085	www.jollyharbour-marina.com/real.html jollyhbradv@candw.ag
TBS Realties	PO Box 1557, St John's, Antigua, West Indies	+268 562 7653	http://tbsrealties.com/ tbs@tbsrealties.com
Antigua Estates	PO Box 118, Jolly Harbour, Antigua, West Indies	+268 562 56 22/24	www.antiguavillas.uk.com

Letting agents:

Name	Address	Tel	Web
TBS Realties	PO Box 1557, St John's, Antigua, West Indies	+268 562 7653	http://tbsrealties.com/ tbs@tbsrealties.com

Barbados, St James, Turtle Beach

Country data

Population	0.275 million
Population growth	0.460%
Land area	430 sq km
Currency and exchange rate	1 Barbadian dollar (Bds$) = 100 cents (~0.279 GBP)
GDP-PPP method	US$2,818.0 millions
GDP growth	−2.550%
GDP per head	$US10,235.0 thousands per person
Financial	**Interest rate** 7.5% · **Inflation rate** 1.50%
National bank	Central Bank of Barbados
Political	The British monarch is Head of State and is represented in Barbados by a Governor General who is advised by the Cabinet and appoints the Prime Minister. The legislature comprises the Governor General, a Senate and the House of Assembly. The Barbados economy has long been used to political and social stability. It is an independent state within the commonwealth. At the moment, the legal system is based on the common law with the final appeal resting with the UK Privy Council. However, this is set to be replaced by the Caribbean Court of Justice.
Social security	Yes
Languages	English
Customaries	Social attitudes, like administration and architecture, tend to echo the British provincial market town. However, the optimistic attitude, laid-back manner and wonderful sense of humour of the Bajans are appreciated by tourists. Casual wear is acceptable in most places. Dressing for dinner in hotels and restaurants is suggested. There are numerous festivals and sporting occasions throughout the year.
Ethnic make-up	African 80.0%; other 16.0%; European 4.0%

Tax	Income Tax			Capital Gains Tax
	Taxable income	Tax on lower amount	Rate on excess	Capital gains are not subject to tax and capital losses are not deductible.
	Exceeding (BDS $) / Not exceeding (BDS $)	(BDS $)	%	
	0 — 24,200	0	25	
	24,200 — –	6,050	40	
	Non-residents are taxed the same as residents except on dividends payments and management payments. Please speak to Barbados government services for more up to date information.			
Description	The Barbados economy traditionally relied on sugar production, but persistent low market prices forced the government to diversify. Most effort has been on tourism, the largest employer on the island. However, after some steady growth over the last decade, there has been some contraction of the economy. The government has launched initiatives to boost the tourism sector. Other major industries are offshore financial services, light manufacturing and component assembly. Major trading partners are the UK, the US, Trinidad and Tobago, Venezuela, Japan, Jamaica and Canada.			

Local data

Investor profile	Holiday investor; retirement investor				
Category	Bronze				
Population	Total 13,000			British 200	
Climate	Hours of sunshine per day in summer	Average rainfall per year	Average temperature January	Average temperature July	Average water temperature
	11	30 days	26°C/79°F	30°C/86°F	23°C
Proximity to	**Airport:** 10 miles from the Grantley Adams International Airport. **Beach:** Amazing beaches everywhere on the island. **Nearest city:** Bridgetown				
Restaurants and bars	It's all here from fine-dining restaurants specializing in award winning cuisine to the very casual serving good food. Barbados is home to some of the world's top 50 restaurants. Turtle Beach is also a few minutes drive away from St Lawrence Gap with its bustling nightlife, and very close to the cosmopolitan town of Bridgetown, which has a diverse array of bars and nightlife.				

Sports and leisure facilities	Tennis, golf, sailing, snorkelling, aquacycling, kayaking, banana boats, sailing, water-skiing, reef fishing and windsurfing.
Transport	**Public transport:** Public buses run regularly to most places on the island. Taxis are plentiful but not particularly cheap. They are also not metered, so agree the fare with the driver in advance of setting off. **Roads:** In good condition. Many car hire services available.
Crime rate	Very low
Main types of employment	Service catering for tourists
Future plans	Further development of tourist sights and activities.
Yield range	5–7%

Type of property	Entry price	Rent – peak	Rent – off peak	Average annual yield
2 bed apartment	£180,000	£1000	£900	6.3%
3 bed apartment	£230,000	£1300	£1100	6.2%
3 bed townhouse	£220,000	£1300	£1100	6.5%
Detached	£245,000	£1300	£1000	5.9%

Demand for letting	Peak Very high		Off peak Very high

Finance and leisure scores:	Financial (out of 5) 1	Leisure (out of 5) 5	Total (out of 10) 6

Flights scheduled from	Gatwick, Heathrow, Manchester

Typical costs of flights	Peak £1100+	Off peak £500–1000

Operators	British Airways, Virgin Atlantic, Caribbean Airways, BWIA Flights, American Airlines, Air Canada

Description	A beautiful stretch of coastline now known as the 'platinum' coast. Here you will see the most obvious signs of opulence, where land is worth more than US $3 million an acre and the rich and famous have made their stake in paradise.
	    I have included this in our hotlist as everyone has heard of Barbados and dreams of visiting it. The rental market has remained competitive hence rental values have been pushed down. However, property prices have risen steadily above worldwide averages and will do so in the long term future.
	    St James is one of the areas you can expect a better yield but only enough to justify it as a holiday or retirement home. You will rent out the property in no time and there are plenty of reputable letting agents. Expect to cover all your costs on a repayment mortgage and look forward to getting a holiday or retirement home for free in 25 years!

Hot website	www.caribzonescaribbean.com/stjamesbchspon.html

▶

Estate agents:			
Name	**Address**	**Tel**	**Web**
Jennifer Alleyne Ltd	Molyneux Plantation, St James, Barbados	(246) 432 1159	www.jalbarbados.com info@jalbarbados.com
AAAltman Real estate	Derricks, St James – West Coast office, Barbados	246 432 0840	www.aaaltman.com realestate@ aaaltman.com
Elegant Properties Realty	Sandy Lane, St James, Barbados	246 432 0221	info@elegant propertiesrealty.com
Letting agents:			
Name	**Address**	**Tel**	**Web**
AAAltman Real Estate	Derricks, St James – West Coast office, Barbados	246 432 0840	www.aaaltman.com realestate@ aaaltman.com
Angler Apartments	Clarke's Rd.#1, Derricks, St James 170209, Barbados		www.barbadosahoy. com/angler/

Mexico, Cancun

Country data	
Population	101.9 million
Population growth	1.52 %
Land area	1,923,040 sq km
Currency and exchange rate	1 new Mexican peso (Mex$) = 100 centavos (~0.048 GBP)
GDP-PPP method	US$861,294.0 millions
GDP growth	−1.800 %
GDP per head	US$8,454.0 thousands per person
Financial	Interest rate 7.09% Inflation rate 5%
National bank	Banco de Mexico
Political	Mexico is a federal republic with the president having executive power and appointing the cabinet. After 71 years of rule by the Partido Revolucionario Institucional (PRI) the right-of-centre Partido de Accion Nacional (PAN) was elected. However, PAN did not gain a landslide and the PRI still hold a strong majority of Mexico's 31 states, especially in the south. President Fox announced that he was committed to modernising Mexico with a view to a new, pluralist Mexican government. His key policies included fiscal reform, tackling rising crime, tackling drug trafficking and associated violence, major changes to make Mexican politics less centralised, addressing human rights issues and raising educational standards.
Social security	Yes
Languages	Spanish; various Mayan dialects
Customaries	Handshaking is the most common form of greeting. Casual sportswear is acceptable for daytime dress throughout the country. At beach resorts, dress is very informal for men and women, but do remember that Roman Catholicism is the prevailing religion of most Mexicans and respect should be maintained in the cities and villages. Mexicans regard friendship and relationships as the most important thing in life next to religion and are not afraid to show their emotions. Local customs and traditions are of high importance for residents and this should be remembered.
Ethnic make-up	Mestizo 60.0%; Indigenous 30.0%; European descent 9.0%; Other 1.0%

▶

Tax	Income Tax			Capital Gains Tax
	Non-residents are taxed on Mexican-source income only.			Capital gains are not subject to a separate tax, but are included in ordinary income and **taxed at the** income rates as displayed
	Residents (as of 2002)			
	Taxable income (P)		Tax on lower amount	Rate on excess
	Exceeding (P)	Not exceeding (P)	(P)	%
	0	5,211.90	0	3
	5,211.90	44,235.83	156.30	10
	44,235.83	77,740.37	4,058.70	17
	77,740.37	90,369.77	9,754.62	25
	90,369.77	108,197.2	12,911.9	32
	108,197.2	218,218.2	18,616.7	33
	218,218.2	636,169.8	54,923.5	34
	636,169.8	–	197, 026	35
	Non-residents			
	Taxable income (P)		Tax on lower amount	Rate on excess
	Exceeding (P)	Not exceeding (P)	(P)	%
	0	125,900	0	20
	125,900	1,000,000	0	15
	1,000,000	–	131,115	30
Description	Major industries: manufacturing, agriculture, commerce, transport and communication, oil and gas, tourism, financial service and electricity. Major trading partner: the USA and trade links with Canada, Germany, China, Japan, Spain and the Netherlands.			

Description (continued)

Major industries: manufacturing, agriculture, commerce, transport and communication, oil and gas, tourism, financial service and electricity. Major trading partner: the USA and trade links with Canada, Germany, China, Japan, Spain and the Netherlands.

The agricultural sector does not play a dominating role as it did until a couple of decades ago.

Mexico still has many structural problems to tackle as it seeks to modernise the economy and raise living standards. However, with the sluggish performance of the economy and divided congress, there is little scope for this in the immediate future.

The Mexican economy is heavily linked to the US economy despite the 33 free trade agreements (FTAs) it has including with the EU, central American countries, Israel and most recently Japan. The USA and Mexican *maquiladoras*, specialist assembly plants based in Northern Mexico, rely almost entirely on the US market. The UK is the largest investor in Mexico after the USA.

Local data				
Investor profile	Cash & equity investor; pension investor; downshifter investor; business investor			
Category	Silver			
Population	Total 457,000		British 2,000	
Climate	Hours of sunshine per day in summer	Average rainfall per year	Average temperature January	Average temperature July	Average water temperature
	10	50 ins	23°C/74°F	28°C/84°F	21°C
Proximity to	**Airport:** Cancun International Airport is 8km (5 miles) south of Cancun City or you can arrive by sea. **Beach:** Playa del Carmen, Chichen Itza and Mexico's Riviera Maya **Nearest city:** The islands of Isla Mujeres, Isla Contoy and Cozumel are the three most visited destinations			
Restaurants and bars	Nightlife in Cancun is world famous. After dining out the party is just beginning. Options include art and culture exhibitions, jazz clubs, salsa bars, reggae and rock. Tropical rhythms abound with live bands from Puerto Rico and Cuba. Most discos open about 10 pm and have different promotions every night.			
Sports and leisure facilities	Cancun offers a great variety: snorkelling, diving, fishing, water skiing, jet skiing, swimming, submarine trips, and much more. Cancun also offers the opportunity of exploring the many lagoon systems and *cenotes* (sink holes). Golf courses are sprouting up all along the coast. You can play in Cancun, Riviera Maya, and Puerto Aventuras, and a new course is going in on Isla Cozumel. Tennis courts are scattered about Quintana Roo; the large hotels at Cancun, Akumal, Cozumel and Puerto Aventuras have them. Bring your own racquet.			
Transport	**Public transport:** The bus system is very dependable and a great way to get between the city and the beaches with stops dotted throughout. **Roads:** Taxis are everywhere. You can also rent a car, moped or bicycle.			
Crime rate	Cancun is a relatively safe city, with less crime than in most small cities across the US. Petty theft is the most common crime, and violent crimes are rare.			
Main types of employment	Tourism is a thriving industry and sustains most of the city's economy.			
Future plans	Mexico's fastest growing resort is even now engaged in several projects, a continuation of the Mexican government's Cancun Master Plan, and a programme for growth that is ecologically sensitive. An undeveloped area southwest of the hotel zone, towards the airport, is poised for more hotels, housing, golf courses and a modern hospital. North of the hotel zone, Puerto Cancun is earmarked for construction: a luxury marina with low-rise hotels and waterfront properties.			

▶

Yield range	11–25%			
Type of property	Entry price	Rent – peak	Rent – off peak	Average annual yield
2 bed apartment	£40,000	£1000	£700	25%
3 bed apartment	£100,000	£1300	£800	13.2%
3 bed townhouse	£70,000	£1300	£800	18.8%
Detached	£135,000	£1500	£1000	11.1%
Demand for letting	Peak Extremely high		Off peak Very high	
Finance and leisure scores	Financial (out of 5) 4	Leisure (out of 5) 4	Total (out of 10) 8	
Flights scheduled from	Regular flights available from all major cities throughout the UK			
Typical cost of flights	Peak £500–£700		Off peak £410–£600	
Operators	Continental, American Airlines, Delta, Air France. AeroMexico, no direct flights.			
Description	Warm white sand beaches, crystal indigo seas, romantic Caribbean nights, world-class hotels, restaurants and nightlife; does all of this sound too good to be true? World-renowned fishing, diving and snorkelling, archaeological sites dating back thousands of years, a balmy tropical climate and water sports galore, and yet Cancun remains a tranquil retreat where you can relax along the peaceful shore of the Caribbean. Yields are great and can weather the 7%+ interest rate. Based on the research we did and the information presented above capital growth prospects will be low in the short term but will gather pace in the medium term. The economy is contracting but this is a temporary blip. Expect the economy to do a u-turn in the next two years.			
Hot website	http://www.allaboutcancun.com/			

Estate agents:

Name	Address	Tel	Web
María Elinda Múgica, Century 21 –	Av. Tulum – Centro	52 (998) 884-1144	realestate.mayan group.com
Arce International Costa Maya Realtors Mayan Group	Av. Coba 30 – Centro; Cancun, Quintana Roo	52 (998) 884-2251 52 (998) 887 71 35	elinda@mayan group.com
Lemmus	Cancun Business Centre, Local G-9, Blvd. 77500, Cancun, Q. Roo	52 (988) 3-20-10	www.lemmus.com

Letting agents:			
Name	**Address**	**Tel**	**Web**
María Elinda Múgica, Mayan Group	Cancun, Quintana Roo	52 998 887 71 35	realestate. mayangroup.com elinda@mayan group.com
Lemmus	Cancun Business Centre, Local G-9, Blvd. 77500, Cancun, Q. Roo	52 (988) 3 20 10	www.lemmus.com

Panama, Panama City, Costa Blanca

Country data

Population	2.85 million
Population growth	1.33%
Land area	75,990 sq km
Currency and exchange rate	1 balboa (B$) = 100 centesimos (~0.55GBP)
GDP-PPP method	US$20,215.0 millions
GDP growth	−1.020%
GDP per head	US$7,104.0 thousands per person

Financial	Interest rate 4.97%	Inflation rate 1%

National bank	National Bank of Panama – offshore banking
Political	Panama's constitution dates from 1972 and was reformed in 1983 and 1994. The president is head of both state and government, and appoints the cabinet.
Social security	Yes
Languages	Spanish (official), English
Customaries	Men and women shake hands in Panama and social kisses on one cheek are also exchanged. Late night parties with dinner served at 2200 or 2300 are common. Panama is an eclectic country, with a ready acceptance of immigrants from all over the world. Public celebrations therefore express the hybrid nature of its diverse cultures. Although once part of Colombia, Panamanian culture and traditions are uniquely its own and show Caribbean rather than South American influence. However, there is little interchange between different social and ethnic groups. Do not take photos without permission, especially of Indians.
Ethnic make-up	Mestizo and other mixed ethnicities 70.0%; West Indian or Caribbean 14.0%; Spanish or other European 10.0%; Indigenous Indian; 10.0%

Tax	Income Tax			Capital Gains Tax
	Taxable income		Tax on lower amount	Rate on excess	Capital gains are taxed at the rates for ordinary income.
	Exceeding (B/.)	Not exceeding (B/.)	(B/.)	%	
	0	3,000	0	0	
	3,000	3,250	0	52	
	3,250	4,000	130	4	
	4,000	6,000	160	6.5	
	6,000	10,000	290	11	
	10,000	15,000	730	16.5	
	15,000	20,000	1,555	19	
	20,000	30,000	2,505	22	
	30,000	40,000	4,705	27	
	40,000	50,000	7,405	30	
	50,000	200,000	10,405	33	
	200,000	–	59,905	30	

Description	Panama historically has had one of the most stable economies in Latin America and unlike other Central American countries, does not rely on primary commodities. The service sector contributes roughly 70% to overall GDP, agriculture 10%, industry 12% and construction 7%. Incomes are higher than average around that area. According to the UN, however, this is heavily skewed as 40% of the population lives in poverty. Major trading partners: the US, Nicaragua, Costa Rica and Sweden. The country is aware that it must pursue structural reform to improve the country's overall competitiveness and attract foreign investment.

Local data

Investor profile	Cash & equity investor; pension investor; holiday investor; retirement investor; downshifter investor; business investor
Category	Bronze

Population	Total 450,000	British 1,500

Climate	Hours of sunshine per day in summer	Average rainfall per year	Average temperature January	Average temperature July	Average water temperature
	10	The rainy season is from April– December. Heaviest rains fall in November ~ 570mm	21°C	31°C	25°C

Proximity to	Airport: Tucumen International Airport is 17 mi/28 km northeast of Panama City and about 25 minutes by car.

	Beach: There are amazing beaches surrounding Panama City along the Costa Blanca **Nearest city:** Balboa
Restaurants and bars	Panama has both oceans hugging its coasts, so you must have seafood! Seafood is in great abundance, especially on the islands. *Pargo rojo* (red snapper) is particularly good, as is sea bass. There are a wide variety of international (Chinese, Italian, etc.) and speciality restaurants (kosher, vegetarian, etc), which are generally very good. You can also find US-style fast food and first-rate gourmet restaurants.
Sports and leisure facilities	Panama City is described as 'a bargainer's paradise' or 'a shopping Mecca'. Because of numerous free trade zones, shopping is the second most popular occupation in the city. Ecotourism, water sports, fishing, golfing, jungle-trekking, horse riding. Boat trips on the Panama Canal are one of Panama's major tourist attractions and there are various types of tours available. Crocodiles, birds and other animals living along the banks and in the surrounding jungle can be observed.
Transport	**Public transport:** The bus is cheap as a form of public transportation. If you need to get faster (almost half of the time) to your destination, you can take the *expressos* which are a lot comfier, roomier and nicer! However, taxis are the best way to get around town. A rail link runs between Puerto Armuelles and David. **Roads:** The Pan-American Highway links Panama with Costa Rica. Routes to Colombia are not generally recommended.
Crime rate	Common street crime has always been prevalent in Panama City and Colón, but poverty as a result of the disrupted economy has worsened the situation. Visitors are warned specifically to avoid locally known hotbeds of crime.
Main types of employment	Service sector and tourism
Future plans	Panama has one of the best economic futures in Latin America. Like Chile, Panama has the potential to raise its people's standard of living above developing nation status in the near future. While private education is good, public education needs continued improvement to prepare young Panamanians for the many jobs that will be created in the sophisticated service sector.
Yield range	8–10%

Type of property	Entry price	Rent – peak	Rent – off peak	Average annual yield
2 bed apartment	£18,000	£150	£110	8.6%
3 bed apartment	£25,000	£240	£180	10%
3 bed townhouse	£23,000	£230	£180	10%
Detached	£30,000	£240	£200	8.8%

▶

Demand for letting	Peak High		Off peak High	
Finance and leisure scores	Financial (out of 5) 3	Leisure (out of 5) 3	Total (out of 10) 6	
Flights scheduled from	London Airports, Manchester, Birmingham, Dublin			
Typical cost of flights	Peak £620–750		Off peak £500–620	
Operators	National airline – Copa, Continental, American Airlines, Delta Airlines, Iberia Airlines			
Description	Panama is one of the most diverse countries in Central America. With pristine rainforest, colonial cities, undeveloped beaches, incredible wildlife, indigenous tribes and one of the greatest engineering feats in the world, Panama is set to become one of the most interesting destinations in Central America. Still in its infancy, the Panamanian tourism infrastructure is already well organised and can offer a huge variety of activities to tempt all tastes, from sightseeing to relaxing, hiking to white water rafting or snorkelling. Entry prices are low, however so are the rents. If the property is going to double up as a holiday home then ensure you furnish it well and get a good agent. This way you will ensure that you get the highest rent possible and have an enjoyable stay. Capital growth will occur, higher than the UK average, as soon as the media start dropping Panama as the new hotspot – which will happen! Get in early while property prices are cheap.			
Hot website	http://panama-information.executivehotel-panama.com			

Estate agents:

Name	Address	Tel	Web
Altos del Maria	Altos del María, Apartado, Postal 8-125, Panamá 8	+ (507) 260 4813	www.altosdelmaria.com/ Lnaar@grupomelo.com
Buena Vista Realty			www.bvrealty-panama.com bvrealty@cwp.net.pa
Mayhew Cook Investments	22 Canfield Rd, Panama City	+(507) 236 8303	www.panama-beachfront-realestate.com info@mayhewcook.com
Arango Arquitectos	Apartado 5318, Panamá 5	+ (507) 300 2336 + (507) 300 2337 + (507) 300 2339	http://www.arangoarq.com info@arangoarq.com

▶

Letting agents:			
Name	**Address**	**Tel**	**Web**
Mayhew Cook Investments	22 Canfield Rd, Panama City	+(507) 236 8303	www.panama-beachfront-realestate.com info@mayhewcook.com
Arango Arquitectos	Apartado 5318, Panamá 5	+ (507) 300 2336 + (507) 300 2337 + (507) 300 2339	http://www.arangoarq.com info@arangoarq.com

USA, Orlando, Florida		
Country data		
Population	284.9 million	
Population growth	1.24%	
Land area	9,166,600 sq km	
Currency and exchange rate	US dollar (~0.548 GBP)	
GDP-PPP method	US$9,022,081.0 millions	
GDP growth	−0.930%	
GDP per head	US$31,665.0 per person	
Financial	**Interest rate** 1.67%	**Inflation rate** 1.6%
National bank	Board of Governors of the Federal Reserve System (Washington) Federal Reserve Bank of New York	
Political	The chief executive of the United States is the President, who is elected to a four-year term. A President may be elected to only two terms and is also Commander-in-Chief of the armed forces. The President's powers are extensive but not unlimited. As the chief formulator of national policy, the President proposes legislation to Congress and may veto any bill passed by Congress. The Congress comprises two chambers – the Senate and the House of Representatives. The USA is a Federal Republic with 50 States and has close associations with the Commonwealth of Puerto Rico, Guam and the US Virgin Islands and exercises trusteeship on behalf of the UN over several Pacific Island groups.	
Social security	Yes	
Languages	Hundreds of languages are spoken in the United States. English and Spanish are the major spoken languages in the United States today. Bilingualism is commonplace.	
Customaries	Shaking hands is the usual form of greeting. The wide variety of national origins and the USA's relatively short history has resulted in numerous cultural and traditional customs living alongside each other. In large cities, people of the same ethnic background often live within defined communities. Gun ownership by civilians is considered part of American heritage. Smoking is becoming increasingly unpopular in the USA and is often considered offensive. It is banned in all restaurants in California and New York City, but in infamous Las Vegas you can find ashtrays in places such as telephones booths.	
Ethnic make-up	European descent 83.5%; African descent 12.4%; Asian descent 3.3%; Amerindian .8% Note that Latinos and Hispanics may fall into any of the ethnic categories listed above.	

▶

Tax	Income Tax				Capital Gains Tax
	Married filling joint return				Net capital gain income is taxed at ordinary rates, except that the maximum rate for long-term gains is limited to 20% (10% for individuals)
	Taxable income ($)		Tax on lower amount	Rate on excess	
	Exceeding ($)	Not exceeding ($)	($)	%	
	0	12,000	0	10	
	12,000	46,700	1,200	15	
	46,700	112,850	6,405	27	
	112,850	171,950	24,266	30	
	171,950	307,050	41,996	35	
	307,050	–	89,280	38.6	
	Married filling separate return				
	Taxable income ($)		Tax on lower amount	Rate on excess	
	Exceeding ($)	Not exceeding ($)	($)	%	
	0	6,000	0	10	
	6,000	23,350	600	15	
	23,350	56,425	3,202	27	
	56,425	85,975	12,133	30	
	85,975	153,525	20,998	35	
	153,525	–	44,640	38.6	
	Head of household				
	Taxable income ($)		Tax on lower amount	Rate on excess	
	Exceeding ($)	Not exceeding ($)	($)	%	
	0	10,000	0	10	
	10,000	37,450	1000	15	
	37,450	96,700	5,118	27	
	96,700	156,600	21,115	30	
	156,600	307,050	39,085	35	
	307,050	–	91,742	38.6	

▶

Single individual			
Taxable income ($)		Tax on lower amount	Rate on excess
Exceeding ($)	Not exceeding ($)	($)	%
0	6,000	0	10
6,000	27,950	600	15
27,950	67,700	3,892	27
67,700	141,250	14,625	30
141,250	307,050	36,690	35
307,050	–	94,720	38.6

Description	The US economy is the world's largest, most powerful and most diverse. As the leading industrial power and most technologically advanced in the world, some of its key industries are petroleum, steel, motor vehicles, aerospace, telecommunications, chemicals, electronics, consumer goods, mining and food processing. Toward the close of 2000, many 'dot-com' industries plunged into bankruptcy. The USA's technology sector went into decline and the country found itself in recession. The events of September 2001 added to the pessimistic outlook for the economy, as several industries suffered a sudden fall in demand. The internationally controversial war on Iraq has also threatened many trade friendships and lowered the value of the US dollar, although the USA's economic might has been maintained. The USA's most important trade relationship is with Canada. The two countries concluded a free trade agreement in 1989: this accord formed the basis for the North American Free Trade Agreement (NAFTA), to which Mexico became a signatory in 1992.

Local data

Investor profile	Cash & equity investor; pension investor; holiday investor; retirement investor; downshifter investor; business investor
Category	Gold

Population	Total 200,000	British 5,000

Climate	Hours of sunshine per day in summer	Average rainfall per year	Average temperature January	Average temperature July	Average water temperature
	9	35 days	22°C	33°C	25°C

Proximity to:	**Airport:** Orlando International Airport – 7 miles south of Orlando
	Beach: Many beaches on either side of Orlando and easily accessible
	Nearest city: Kissimee

Restaurants and bars	You can get any kind of food in Orlando and the number of restaurants in the region is amazing. With such a wide variety of choice and the hearty portions provided, you're sure never to be spoilt for choice. There are also endless bars, each offering different nights and themes. You are sure never to get bored of the vibrancy of the nightlife.
Sports and leisure facilities	Orlando Magic is based here if you fancy watching the odd basketball game. Springtime is great for a spot of baseball and the excellent world-class golfing greens are an excellent way of winding away the hours. There are also many places nearby the Orlando area where you can go diving and sailing. The waters of Florida are also renowned for great surf and classes are easily available.
Transport	**Public Transport:** Orlando has excellent public transport including the cheap I-Ride Tram-Bus service. You definitely do not need a car to get around. Taxis are also readily available. **Roads:** Excellent links to the rest of the US.
Crime rate	Relatively low, yet precautions must be taken as per usual in cities.
Main types of employment	Services, industry, tourism
Future plans	To improve and maintain the tourism industry
Yield range	16–22%

Type of property	**Entry price**	**Rent – peak**	**Rent – off peak**	**Average annual yield**
2 bed apartment	£52,000	£1000	£900	22%
3 bed apartment	£70,000	£1200	£800	17%
3 bed townhouse	£75,000	£1300	£900	17%
Detached	£90,000	£1400	£900	16%

Demand for letting	**Peak** Very high		**Off peak** Quite high	

Finance and leisure scores	**Financial** (out of 5) 5	**Leisure** (out of 5) 5	**Total** (out of 10) 10

Flights scheduled from	London, Birmingham, Manchester and all other major cities

Typical cost of flights	**Peak** £700–1100	**Off peak** £400–550

Operators	Northwest, Delta, British Airways, Continental, US airways, AER Lingus, Air France, United, Lufthansa, Iceland Air, Air Canada, American Airlines, Monarch
Description	Orlando is one of the world's premier travel destinations. More than 35 million people visit the area every year, enjoying the many attractions, beaches, and events that make Central Florida a great place to visit and live. This is my personal favourite. Low borrowing costs and high yields mean BIG profits! If you did a draft profit and loss of a prospective property you would find that you would make a lot of money. I suggest you invest in the high tenant demand areas. The property prices in

▶

	these areas will be higher than the entry prices stated above so will affect yields but not by much – a lot more can be had by paying that little bit more. Finance for properties in the USA is easy to get. Loan To Values are currently at 70% max so you will need more to put down than you would if you were buying in the UK but the yields compensate for this. The dollar rate is very favourable at the minute so strike now!
Hot website	http://www.ci.orlando.fl.us/

Estate agents:

Name	Address	Tel	Web
Florida Invest	4700 Millenia Blvd, Suite 175, Orlando, FL 32839	(407) 210 3843	info@floridainvest.us www.floridainvest.us
Steve Walke	Re/Max Town Centre, 315 E. Robinson Street, Suite 415, Orlando, FL. 32801	407 399 5674	Steve@MyOrlando RealEstatePro.com
Eurus International Realty			http://www.eurus-realty.com/ jurdy@eurus-realty.com
Brixton Development	2003 12730 New Brittany Blvd., Suite 205, Fort Myers, Florida 33907	239 425 6500	sales@brixton development.com www.brixton development.com/

Letting agents:

Name	Address	Tel	Web
Florida Invest	4700 Millenia Blvd, Suite 175, Orlando, FL 32839	(407) 210 3843	info@floridainvest.us www.floridainvest.us
Steve Walke	Re/Max Town Centre, 315 E. Robinson Street, Suite 415, Orlando, FL. 32801	407 399 5674	Steve@MyOrlando RealEstatePro.com

Oceania

Australia, Queensland
New Zealand, Mount Maunganui, Leigh

Australia, Queensland

Country data	
Population	19.36 million
Population growth	1.01%
Land area	7,617,930 sq km
Currency and exchange rate	1 Australian Dollar (A$) = 100 cents (~0.382557 GBP)
GDP-PPP method	US$412,230.0 millions
GDP growth	1.58%
GDP per head	US$21,296 per person
Financial	**Interest rate** 5.25 % **Inflation rate** 2 %
National Bank	Reserve Bank of Australia
Political	The Commonwealth of Australia is a constitutional monarchy with a parliamentary democracy. It consists of a federation of six states and two territories. Each state has its own constitution, government, administration and judiciary. The governor general represents and is appointed by the British sovereign. The role is largely ceremonial, but he has the power to dissolve parliament or the government and call new elections. Day-to-day executive responsibility is held by the national government, composed of a cabinet formed by the party with a majority in the House of Representatives.
Social security	Yes
Languages	English, indigenous languages, various languages spoken by immigrant communities
Customaries	Australians tend to be informal and first names are quickly adopted. Shaking hands is the customary greeting. Business, with traditional blunt, straight-to-the-point talk, is often conducted over lunch or dinner accompanied by local wines and beers. Most restaurants forbid smoking. Visitors often complain about bureaucracy and patience is required in dealing with government departments and large corporations. Australia has strict drink and driving laws. Police conduct random roadside breath tests and penalties can be severe.
Ethnic make-up	Caucasian 92.0%; Asian 7.0%; Aboriginal 1.0%

▶

Tax	Income Tax				Capital Gains Tax
	Applicable to Australian residents:				Capital gains realised by non-residents on capital gains tax assets are subject to Australian tax only if the assets have the necessary connection to Australia. This includes Australian real estate.
	Taxable income		Tax on lower amount	Rate on excess	
	Exceeding (A$)	Not exceeding (A$)	(A$)	(%)	
	0	6,000	0	0*	
	6,000	20,000	0	17	
	20,000	50,000	2,380	30	
	50,000	60,000	11,380	42	
	60,000	-	15,580	47	
	Applicable to non-residents				
	Taxable income		Tax on lower amount	Rate on excess	
	Exceeding (A$)	Not exceeding (A$)	(A$)	(%)	
	0	20,000	0	29	
	20,000	50,000	5,800	30	
	50,000	60,000	14,800	42	
	60,000	–	19,800	47	

Description	Australia has a very diverse economy and a high standard of living with the service sector accounting for almost three-quarters of GDP. Considerable investment in export-oriented mining and energy projects led to a growth in coal and iron ore exports, but also contributed to a rapid rise in gross external debt. Most Australian manufacturing is concentrated in processing mineral products and iron, steel and engineering industries. Also exports wool, beef and live sheep.
	The most important development in the economy in recent years has been a shift in trading patterns away from Britain and Europe towards the Pacific Rim – 60% of Australian exports are now sold in that region. Major trading partners: Japan, USA, South Korea, Taiwan, Singapore, New Zealand, China and then the EU nations.

Local data		
Investor profile	Cash & equity investor; pension investor; holiday investor; retirement investor; downshifter investor; business investor	
Category	Bronze	
Population	Total 3,635,121	British 35,000

Climate	Hours of sunshine per day in summer	Average rainfall per year	Average temperature January	Average temperature July	Average water temperature
	10	400mm	25.2°C	15.7°C	20°C

Proximity to	**Airport:** Brisbane, Cairns and Townsville have international airports, there are several domestic airports within Queensland as well.
	Beach: 7,400 km of coastline allow for access to the beach from almost anywhere.
	Nearest city: The main cities are Brisbane, Cairns and Townsville

Restaurants and bars	Queensland has a wide variety of restaurants from five star to pleasant BYOs (bring your own alcohol) in the suburbs. Most BYO restaurants charge a small amount for corkage and glasses.

Sports and leisure facilities	Surfing at southern beaches, calm clear water at northern beaches, warm water all year round, lifeguards and safe conditions, sun, clean, soft sand, clear water. A huge number of beaches to choose from, the most popular being Surfer's Paradise. Great fishing. Water sports such as windsurfing, sailing, water skiing, kite surfing.

Transport	**Public transport:** Queensland has good bus, train, plane, ferry, taxi, hire car or caravan facilities centred mainly around Brisbane, Cairns and Townsville.
	Roads: Excellent road links allow for ease of travel to almost anywhere

Crime rate	Lower than the Australian average

Main types of employment	Queensland is a cosmopolitan state in Australia with a range of employment opportunities both professional and for self-employment in tourism. This sector accounts for the second largest contribution to Queensland's GDP. Commercial services are available abundantly in Brisbane, Cairns and Townsville, the main cities in Queensland.

Future plans	Opportunities in the years ahead will arise from observing the moves made by the influential baby boomer generation. A major finding of the report is that baby boomers will continue to be key drivers of the residential property markets for the next decade and beyond as they look for lifestyle and community living. This trend has already begun with a move to second homes or holiday homes in coastal areas. These areas now have all the younger lifestyle attributes which include food and wine.

Yield range	6–8 %

Type of property	Entry price	Rent – peak	Rent – off peak	Average annual yield
2 bed apartment	£40,000	£250	£250	7.5%
3 bed apartment	£55,000	£300	£300	6.5%
3 bed townhouse	£70,000	£360	£360	6.1%
Detached	£90,000	£550	£550	7.3%

▶

Demand for letting	Peak Excellent		Off peak Very good
Finance and leisure scores	Financial (out of 5) 3	Leisure (out of 5) 3	Total (out of 10) 6
Flights scheduled from	All main cities in the UK but cheapest flights are from London		
Typical cost of flights	Peak £500–£1000		Off peak £500–£700
Operators	Most long-haul carriers fly to Queensland, and include stops in their countries of origin at a special discounted fare. These include Asian Airlines, Royal Brunei Airways, Malaysia Airlines, Singapore Airlines, Thai Airways, Cathay Pacific, Emirates, Air New Zealand and British Airways.		
Description	Australia's fastest growing state is host to five of Australia's 11 World Heritage areas including one of the wonders of the world – the Great Barrier Reef – and access is available from many parts of Queensland. In the city explore shopping and historic precincts, dine on seafood, soak in culture at a museum or art gallery. Head to spectacular Moreton Bay and islands or country hinterland. This is one of the last few areas worth investing in in Australia. Prices are very reasonable and set to boom. I have chosen this area for a great holiday home that can cover its costs whilst you're not there. Expect a good gain over the medium to long term.		
Hot website	www.queenslandholidays.co.uk		

Estate agents

Name	Address	Tel	Web
Australian Property Connection	Shop 23–24, 20 Lake Street, Cairns 4870, QLD	+61 40740 5776	www.austprop connection.com/
Australian Real Estate Direct	37 Front St, Mossman 4873, QLD	+61 7 3893 0360	www.realestate direct.com.au/
Alan McGillivray Real Estate	Shop 23 Surfers International, Hanlan St. Surfers Paradise 4217, QLD	+61 7/55 702300	www.goldcoast units.com.au/
First National Real Estate	89 Hoddle Street, Richmond, Victoria 3121	+61 3 9419 6311	qld@firstnational. com.au www.queensland property.com.au/

Letting agents:			
Name	Address	Tel	Web
SEQ Rents	PO Box 3112, Norman Park, Brisbane, QLD 4170	+61 7 3397 3474	www.seqrents.com.au/
Alan McGillivray Real Estate	Shop 23 Surfers International, Hanlan St. Surfers Paradise 4217, QLD	+61 7/55 702300	www.goldcoastunits. com.au/

New Zealand, Mount Maunganui, Leigh

Country data	
Population	3.86 million
Population growth	1.16%
Land area	268,670 sq km
Currency and exchange rate	1 New Zealand dollar (NZ$) = 100 cents 1 (NZ$) = £0.3414
GDP-PPP method	US$63,559.0 millions
GDP growth	1.32%
GDP per head	US$16,448.0 thousands per person

Financial	Interest rate 5.75%	Inflation rate 2.7%

National bank	Reserve Bank of New Zealand
Political	New Zealand is an independent parliamentary democracy and member of the Commonwealth. Government is based on the UK parliament. The conservative National Party and left-leaning Labour Party have dominated New Zealand political life. The head of state is Queen Elizabeth II. The last elections were held in July 2002.
Social security	Yes
Languages	English (official), Maori
Customaries	Same as western cultures
Ethnic make-up	New Zealand European 75.0%; Maori 10.0%; Asian and others 7.0%; Pacific Islander 4.0%; other European 4.0%

Tax	Income Tax			Capital Gains Tax
	Married persons are taxed separately, not jointly, on all types of income.			New Zealand has no general capital gains tax, although profits from sale of property may be subject to regular income tax as underlined.
	Taxable income (P)		Tax on lower amount	Rate on excess	
	Exceeding (NZ$)	Not exceeding (NZ$)	(NZ$)	%	
	0	38,000	0	19.5	
	38,000	60,000	7,410	33	
	60,000	–	14,670	39	

Description	New Zealand underwent one of the most radical economic transformations of any Western industrialised country, with wholesale privatisation, the abolition of subsidies, tariff barriers and corporate regulations, and the dismantling of many welfare systems. The country is reputed to be among the most open economies in the world, while

▶

	inflation has consistently stayed under the government's 3% target since the mid-1990s. New Zealand is primarily thought of as an agricultural country, but has transformed to an industrialised nation. However, agriculture still accounts for 40% of export income, primarily from wool, meat and dairy, and wood products. Major trading partners: Australia, USA, Japan, China, Germany and the UK. In the long-term, New Zealand will need to reduce its large current account deficit and sustain the growth in productivity.

Local data		

Investor profile	Cash & equity investor; pension investor; holiday investor; retirement investor; downshifter investor; business investor		
Category	Bronze		
Population	**Total** 30,000		**British** 300 or less

Climate	Hours of sunshine per day in summer	Average rainfall per year	Average temperature January	Average temperature July	Average water temperature
		1,200–1,600 mm	12°C	24°C	18°C

Proximity to:	**Airport:** Tauranga Airport is about 2km from Tauranga and just minutes from Mount Maunganui **Beach:** Mount Maunganui Beach **Nearest city:** Tauranga
Restaurants and bars	Nice restaurants at the marina with interesting people. Colourful and aromatic dishes are proudly displayed. Many varieties to choose from: Turkish, seafood, Chinese, Indian, steakhouse, Italian, Japanese, Thai, pizzas, etc. A good selection of bars and pubs line the streets in Mount Maunganui and nearby Tauranga.
Sports and leisure facilities	Mount Maunganui has a multi purpose port, catering for cruise ships and cargo ships as well as a very nice marina for sailboats and launches. The combination of a great climate, a choice of venues as well as the harbour and ocean, makes Mount Maunganui ideal for indoor and outdoor recreation with some of the more daring being dolphin swimming, skydiving, active volcanic island trips, coromandel tours, rafting and surfing.
Transport	**Public transport:** InterCity Coachline operates daily services to Mount Maunganui and the surrounding Bay of Plenty region. Comfortable, air-conditioned transport. Good bus network, and ferries available to get to other smaller islands. **Roads:** Good condition and excellent links to south island.
Crime rate	Low
Main types of employment	Service and sales workers

Future plans	No published information			
Yield range	6–8%			
Type of property	Entry price	Rent – peak	Rent – off peak	Average annual yield
2 bed apartment	£50,000	£250	£250	6%
3 bed apartment	£80,000	£400	£400	6%
3 bed townhouse	£70,000	£500	£400	7.7%
Detached	£85,000	£500	£500	7%

Demand for letting	Peak	Off peak
	Quite High	Moderate to average

Finance and leisure scores	Financial (out of 5)	Leisure (out of 5)	Total (out of 10)
	2	4	6

Flights scheduled from	London Airports and other major cities. Connection flight usually required.	

Typical cost of flights	Peak	Off peak
	£1200–3000	£900–1400

Operators	Cathay Pacific, Air New Zealand, British Airways, Qantas Airways, Virgin Atlantic, Singapore Airlines, Japan Airlines Company

| Description | The mountain of Mount Maunganui, also known to the local Maori people as Mauao, is shrouded in legend and history. It's the dominant geological feature of the Tauranga District, with its conical rocky outline rising 232 metres above sea level. It has been of great importance to local Maori for more than six centuries as a place of occupation and later as a refuge for defence. Mount Maunganui is a wonderful sunny holiday resort, with its prominent volcanic cone that gives it its name. It is popular with surfers.

I had to include somewhere in Australasia as it is so popular with us British! There was only one area (see Queensland below) in Australia worth mentioning as they have had a boom like us in the UK. This area in New Zealand is very affordable with entry prices for 1 bed flats found at £35,000. Obtaining finance for UK residents is very easy at high Loan To Values of up to 80%. Yields are not so great but capital growth prospects are above average as it is one of the last areas yet to boom. |
|---|---|

Hot website	www.mountmaunganui.co.nz/

Estate agents:

Name	Address	Tel	Web
The Reef	178 Marine Parade, Mt Maunganui	+64 7 574 6220	www.thereef.co.nz the.reef@xtra.co.nz
Eastside Real Estate	438 Maunganui Road, Mount Maunganui	+64 7 575 8018	mount@eastreal.co.nz
Harcourts – Central	PO Box 5031, Mount Maunganui	+64 7 575 6384	homelife@wave.co.nz

▶

Letting agents:			
Name	Address	Tel	Web
LJ Hooker – Commercial	PO Box 5418, Mount Maunganui	+64 7 574 3888	bop@ljhcommercial.co.nz

Letting agents:			
Name	Address	Tel	Web
Cutterscove	136 Marine Parade, Mt Maunganui	64 7 575 4136	www.cutterscove.co.nz/ info@cutterscove.co.nz
The Reef	178 Marine Parade, Mt Maunganui	+64 7 574 6220	www.thereef.co.nz the.reef@xtra.co.nz

South America

Brazil, Fortaleza

Brazil, Fortaleza		
Country data		
Population	174.5 million	
Population growth	0.930%	
Land area	8,456,510 sq km	
Currency and exchange rate	1 real (R$) = 100 centavos (~0.172815 GBP)	
GDP-PPP method	US$1,048,754.0 millions	
GDP growth	0.560%	
GDP per head	US$6,011.0 thousands per person	
Financial	**Interest rate** 15%	**Inflation rate** 12.5%
National bank	Banco Central do Brasil	
Political	The present constituency was formulated in 1988. Legislative power rests with the bicameral National Congress. The federal republic consists of 26 states and one federal district. ⁣⁣ The current President Luiz Inacio 'Lula' da Silva, the leader of the Worker's Party, won the 2002 Presidential Elections convincingly. His election represents a vote for change. Lula has pledged to continue his predecessor's commitment to IMF targets and fiscal discipline. He has so far managed to win the confidence of the markets, and has given his full backing to the Central Bank which has increased interest rates to keep control over inflation. But he has also pledged to deliver a better social deal for Brazil's poor by announcing a Zero Hunger campaign with the aim of reaching 1.5 million poor families by the end of the year.	
Social security	Yes	
Languages	Portuguese (official); over 195 indigenous languages; German; Italian; Japanese; Korean; Baltic languages	
Customaries	Handshaking is customary and normal European courtesies are observed. Frequent offers of coffee and tea are customary. Flowers are acceptable as a gift on arrival or following a visit for a meal. A souvenir from the visitor's home country will be well received. Casual wear is normal, particularly during hot weather. Smoking is acceptable unless notified otherwise. The Catholic Church is highly respected in the community. ⁣⁣ There are a number of lavish festivals throughout the year in Brazil, the two most notable being Bahia's Carnival just after Christmas (from December to March) and the Carnival in Rio de Janeiro (February/March), widely regarded as the most spectacular and extravagant in the world.	
Ethnic make-up	European (Portuguese, German, Italian, Spanish, Polish) 53.0%; Mulatto (mixed European and African) 38.0%; African 6.0%; Asian (Japanese) 1.0%; Middle Eastern (Lebanese, Syrian, Turkish) 1.0%; Indigenous (includes 200 small ethno-linguistic groups) and Mestizo (mixed European and Indigenous) 1.0%.	

▶

Tax	Income Tax			Capital Gains Tax
	Federal income tax is levied on taxable income.			Subject to a flat rate of 15%.
	Monthly taxable income			Special exemption given to those who have owned residence for five years or more and if the sale price does not exceed R$440,000.
	Taxable income (R$)		**Tax on lower amount**	**Rate on excess**	
	Exceeding (R$)	**Not exceeding (R$)**	**(R$)**	**%**	
	0	1,058	0	0	
	1,058	2,115	159	15	
	2,115	–	423	27.5	
	Annual taxable income				
	Taxable income (R$)		**Tax on lower amount**	**Rate on excess**	
	Exceeding (R$)	**Not exceeding (R$)**	**(R$)**	**%**	
	0	12,696	0	0	
	12,696	25,380	1,904	15	
	25,380	–	5,077	27.5	
	Non-residents are subject to tax at a flat rate of 25%				
Description	Brazil is the most populated and largest country in South America, with a vast wealth of natural resources. Major industries: agriculture, iron ore and minerals, steel, oil, food, wood, footwear and textiles, automotive, aerospace, electronics and financial services. Main trading partners: the US, UK, Argentina, Chile, Germany, China, Japan, Portugal and France. Brazil also is a major player in the Mercosul common market with Argentina, Paraguay and Uruguay (Bolivia and Chile have association agreements with Mercosul). Recently the Brazilian economy has been unsteady but Lula retained the successful market growth strategies generated by his predecessor. He has also acted on reform to produce high rates of sustainability in areas such as public sector pension system, employment and reforms of tax. The gradual growth of the economy is being slightly overshadowed by high inflation rates, yet prospects for 2005 look better with predicted growth.			

Local data				
Investor profile	Cash & equity investor; pension investor; downshifter investor; business investor			
Category	Bronze			
Population	**Total** 7,400,000		**British** 2000	

Climate	Hours of sunshine per day in summer	Average rainfall per year	Average temperature January	Average temperature July	Average water temperature
	10	130 days	31°C	29°C	27°C

Proximity to	**Airport:** Aeroporto Pinto Martins Fortaleza CE 30 minutes drive from the city
	Beach: Praia Beira Mar, Praia do Futuro and the Beach Park
	Nearest city: (Jericoacoara) and Natal

Restaurants and bars	Fortaleza is well served with good restaurants and you can find many varieties of food ranging from typical Bahian dishes, Italian, Korean and Japanese, with the Kabuki and Moyashi restaurants favoured by travellers and locals.
	As Fortaleza is on the coast, expect to find a plethora of fine seafood restaurants serving feasts throughout the day. There are always places by the beach where you can enjoy some very good crab and sit with your friends listening to live music. There are numerous bars and cafés and places where you can sing and dance!
	There is always something going on in Fortaleza. At the weekends, there are always clubs and bars trying to tempt in the customers, in addition to the fantastic year round concerts packed with famous artists.

Sports and leisure facilities	One of the best places to go windsurfing, if not the best, is near Fortaleza. Take your pick from water sports, dune buggy rides, sand boarding, boat rides, fishing, horseback riding, football and volleyball.

Transport	**Public transport:** Travel to and from Fortaleza is best accomplished by plane or bus or even by boat! Within the city itself, there is a lot of public transport such as buses and taxis. Fortaleza has also introduced an innovative transportation method called MotoTaxi. To use this service, one pays roughly £1 to get anywhere in town by motorcycle.
	Roads: The roads are in excellent condition and provide good travelling links to other cities throughout the country.

Crime rate	Be careful not to accept drinks from strangers. The safest way to travel is using taxis or public bus system. Stay in well-lit areas and take the usual precautions that you would whilst abroad. Also take into consideration that even though Fortaleza is a very modern city, once outside the city things change rapidly.

Main types of employment	Fortaleza does suffer from unemployment, yet fares much better than most other northern states and is the wealthiest city in the Brazilian north east.
	Fortaleza deals mainly in agricultural products such as sugar, coffee, rubber, cotton, rum, rice, beans and fruits in addition to providing tourism and services.
Future plans	The north east of Brazil is starting to see a large increase in international tourism. With flights becoming cheaper, Latin America is becoming a popular destination. The fantastic long-distance bus services offered in Brazil have improved the communications between cities in addition to regular internal flights through domestic carriers.
Yield range	11–18%

Type of property	Entry price	Rent – peak	Rent – off peak	Average annual yield
2 bed apartment	£16,000	£280	£230	18%
3 bed apartment	£31,000	£310	£270	11%
3 bed townhouse	£29,000	£310	£260	11.7%
Detached	£31,000	£320	£280	11.6%

Demand for letting	Peak		Off peak	
	High		Moderately high	

Finance and leisure scores	Financial (out of 5)	Leisure (out of 5)	Total (out of 10)
	3	3	6

Flights scheduled from	Manchester, Birmingham, London Airports and some other major airports. Usually at least one connection flight is required through Milan, Lisbon or Amsterdam from Europe or through Miami in the USA.

Typical cost of flights	Peak	Off peak
	£600–£800	£400–£650

Operators	Varig Air, British Airways, Alitalia, Tap Air, Tam airlines, Air France, Iberia, Lufthansa, United Airlines, Aerolineas Argentina
Description	Fortaleza is the wealthiest city in the Brazilian north east and definitely one of the most beautiful. It is known for its beautiful beaches, the year-round sunshine, soft breeze and rich handicraft. It is a tropical paradise where you can find nice hospitable people and its nightlife is unique. The popular local fishing village of Jericoacoara is a place of great natural beauty. Travellers often delay their departure because they find this such a unique and beautiful part of Brazil.
	Yields are dwarfed by a high interest rate which has been set to control the hyper inflation that the country has experienced. Political reform hints that the interest rate can be lowered significantly as inflation is controlled. When this happens the yields will then make sense. Entry costs are low due to lack of demand and such high borrowing rates. If you can purchase a property for cash then do so and remortgage when the interest rate has fallen below 8%. This is a wild card entry as there is a fair degree of financial risk investing here because of the country's track record.
Hot website	www.jericoacoara.com

Estate agents:			
Name	**Address**	**Tel**	**Web**
Property Bond International Ltd	17/19 Amsterdam Road, Isle of Dogs, Docklands, London E14 3UU	+44 (0) 207 538 0102	www.brazilian-property.co.uk
Fortaleza Houses		+55 85 8805 1953	information@ fortalezahouses.com www.fortalezahouses. com
Flat Shop		+55 85 219 1657	www.cumbuco-beach.com/ Realestate.htm flatshop-cumbuco@ bol.com.br
Brazil Classified			www.brazilclassifieds. com
Letting agents:			
Name	**Address**	**Tel**	**Web**
Fortaleza Houses		+55 85 8805 1953	information@ fortalezahouses.com www.fortalezahouses. com
Flat Shop		+55 85 219 1657	www.cumbuco-beach.com/ Realestate.htm flatshop-cumbuco@ bol.com.br

Sources

The Global Executive – Ernst & Young Global Limited 2004

www.countrywatch.com – Countrywatch

www.bis.org/cbanks.htm – Central Bank websites

www.worldinformation.com – World Information.com

www.fco.gov.uk – Foreign and Commonwealth Office country profiles

biz.yahoo.com/ifc/index.html – Yahoo! International finance centre

www.columbusguides.com – Columbus world travel guide

www.trade.uktradeinvest.gov.uk/ – UK Trade and Investment

www.lonelyplanet.com/ – Lonely Planet Online

www.weatheronline.co.uk – Weather online

www.geohive.com/cd/index.php – Geohive: global statistics

www.archersdirect.co.uk – Archers Direct country information

www.virtualtourist.com – Virtual Tourist

www.nationmaster.com – Nation Master

www.mapzones.com – Map Zones

www.escapeartist.com – The Escape Artist

www.dial4aflight.co.uk – Dial4aflight

If you want to know how … to make money from property

'Many of the world's richest people have made their fortunes from property. Now you can make money from property too – if you are careful. This book will show you how to spot property investment opportunities and how to avoid all the common mistakes. Whether your objective is to add a little to your income in retirement or become a full-time property developer, this book will show you how.'

Adam Walker

How to Make Money from Property

The expert guide to property investment

Adam Walker

'Invest in this book today and make it your first valuable property investment.' – *Amazon review*

'A guide to many different ways of making money from property, from letting a room to buying land for development.' – *landllordzone.co.uk*

'I was already considering investing in the property market…Initially sceptical, I found this book to be my first step on the property investment ladder.'– *Amazon review*

ISBN 1 85703 627 1

If you want to know how ... invest to emigrate

This book discusses the rules, pitfalls and advantages of the world's major immigrant investor programmes – programmes that offer permanent residence through investment schemes designed to attract capital and entrepreneurial skills. It includes the US, the UK, Australia, New Zealand and Canada as well as other frequently sought out locations such as Switzerland, Costa Rica, Malta, Malaysia, Belize and Fiji. This book will enable you to investigate and pursue the options available to you.

Invest to Emigrate

How to gain permanent residence in the country of your choice through international invest-to-emigrate programmes

Henry Liebman

Henry Liebman has practised US immigration law for over 20 years, specialising in visas pertaining to investors. His US experience has given him a wide perspective and insight into other global invest-to-emigrate programmes. His book identifies each country's policies so that the reader can determine whether their own goals fit with those of the host country, the first and most important step to making a successful application.

ISBN 1 85703 994 7

If you want to know how … to retire abroad

'Just because you're retired doesn't mean that you are content to sit back and reminisce about the past. Instead you are determined to live life to the full and fulfil as many of your aspirations as you can. These may well involve spending time in a different – probably warmer – clime for part or even all of the year. This book offers suggestions and advice and also provides a wide range of contacts – from estate agents to embassies, from furniture removers to financial advisers. I hope that this guide will prove indispensable in your decision making, steering you successfully in the right direction.'

Roger Jones

How to Retire Abroad

Your complete guide to a fresh start in the sun

Roger Jones

'Provides advice and hard facts on finding a location, getting there, and coping once you're there – and even contains advice if you decide you want to come back! Invaluable chapters include 'What You Need to Know Before Proceeding' and 'How Much Will It Cost? The appendices are packed with useful addresses and phone numbers.' – *The Mirror*

'…contains much thought-provoking information for those considering spending their golden years abroad.' – *French Property News*

'The guide is an excellent starting point. It represents a very modest investment when one considers the expensive and/or ghastly mistakes that may ensue if important points are overlooked.' – *Living France*

ISBN 1 85703 976 9

How To Books are available through all good bookshops, or you can order direct from us through Grantham Book Services.

Tel: +44 (0)1476 541080

Fax: +44 (0)1476 541061

Email: *orders@gbs.tbs-ltd.co.uk*

Or via our website

www.howtobooks.co.uk

To order via any of these methods please quote the title(s) of the book(s) and your credit card number together with its expiry date.

For further information about our books and catalogue, please contact:

How To Books
3 Newtec Place
Magdalen Road
Oxford OX4 1RE

Visit our web site at

www.howtobooks.co.uk

Or you can contact us by email at *info@howtobooks.co.uk*